# TEACHING SCIENCE in the TWO-YEAR COLLEGE

# TEACHING SCIENCE in the TWO-YEAR COLLEGE

TIMOTHY M. COONEY, EDITOR

An NSTA Press Journals Collection

NATIONAL SCIENCE TEACHERS ASSOCIATION

Arlington, Virginia

NATIONAL SCIENCE TEACHERS ASSOCIATION

Claire Reinburg, Director
Andrew Cocke, Associate Editor
Judy Cusick, Associate Editor
Betty Smith, Associate Editor

JOURNAL OF COLLEGE SCIENCE TEACHING Lauren Beben, Managing Editor
ART AND DESIGN Linda Olliver, Director
NSTA WEB Tim Weber, Webmaster
PERIODICALS PUBLISHING Shelley Carey, Director
PRINTING AND PRODUCTION Catherine Lorrain-Hale, Director
    Nguyet Tran, Assistant Production Manager
    Jack Parker, Desktop Publishing Specialist
PUBLICATIONS OPERATIONS Hank Janowsky, Manager
sciLINKS Tyson Brown, Manager
    David Anderson, Web and Development Coordinator


NATIONAL SCIENCE TEACHERS ASSOCIATION
Gerald F. Wheeler, Executive Director
David Beacom, Publisher

**Teaching Science in the Two-Year College:** An NSTA Press Journals Collection
    NSTA Stock Number: PB180X
05    04    03    4    3    2    1

**Library of Congress Cataloging-in-Publication Data**

Teaching science in the two-year college : an NSTA Press journals
collection / Timothy M. Cooney, Editor.
    p. cm.
A collection of articles from the NSTA journal The journal of college
science teaching.
  ISBN 0-87355-230-X
  1.  Science—Study and teaching (Higher)  I. Cooney, Timothy M. II.
National Science Teachers Association.
  Q181.T3537 2003
  507'.1'1—dc22
                        2003018818

# Contents

# Section III

## Teaching Strategies for the Two-Year College

# Section IV
## Using Information and Communication Technologies

# Introduction

Two-year colleges often have unique missions and goals compared to those of four-year or graduate colleges. Likewise, faculty at these institutions face unique challenges. Mission statements for two-year colleges regularly state that the college is richly diverse, comprehensive, and serves the needs of a specific geographic area. In addition, the college has a commitment to provide an accessible and affordable education through a knowledgeable faculty and staff, a responsive and flexible curriculum, and strong community partnerships. There is a fundamental commitment to teaching and learning excellence in both baccalaureate and career-focused educational programs. Some data indicate that about half of our future science teachers will take their first two years of science at a two-year school.

*Teaching Science in the Two-Year College* examines issues science faculty at two-year colleges frequently face. The articles, drawn from the *Journal of College Science Teaching*, discuss the topics of curriculum, teaching strategies, and the use of educational technologies. The authors provide examples of how they tackled challenges at their institutions.

## The uniqueness of teaching science in the two-year college

The first section offers insights about the uniqueness of teaching in a two-year college. *Hello! Is Anybody Out There?* explores one commonality that exists among many two-year colleges—*isolation,* including the social, financial, and political isolation of community college educators. While schools invest in institutional research, this information too often remains sequestered and unused within the institutional archives. The author provides suggestions on how two-year colleges and faculty can better link for their mutual benefit.

Many times, two-year college students are uncertain about continuing their academic pursuits. *The First Day of Class on a Two-Year Campus* explores student apprehensions regarding science classes, explaining that anxiety about science courses can be attributed to lack of prior knowledge and loss of personal control. The authors discuss student perceptions and how to support and encourage student confidence.

While part-time instructors are not unique to two-year colleges, some of their employment issues are. *Adjunct Faculty* provides a multi-dimensional view of the essential work performed by the part-time faculty and looks at the problems and dilemmas posed by this untenured staff.

*The Graying of Science Faculty in U.S. Colleges and Universities* sheds light on a staffing crisis facing two-year colleges. The authors look at questions such as: Where are the younger faculty who will continue to teach science over the next 20 or 30 years? Who will remain to mentor the younger faculty who will be appointed over the next several years? Will there be enough younger, qualified individuals to fill the need? The article presents a study of age demographics of college science-teaching faculty in the United States, with several recommendations on how to deal with the crisis.

*The Counseling/Science Connection* explains how the counseling department can be a valuable part of the science instructional team. However, the faculty does not always take advantage of this collaborative opportunity. This article explores some of the advantages that can accrue when a classroom teacher teams up with a counselor. The author, a psychological counselor who had worked closely with a classroom teacher, discusses the role of campus counseling services, the developmental needs of two-year college students, and how to seek counseling assistance.

## Curricular issues in the two-year college

Curricular issues in science courses are as common at the two-year college as they are at other post-secondary institutions. While the National Science Education Standards address the K–12 level, they have also generated much interest in two-year colleges. The article *Navigating the Standards* looks at the importance of the Standards for colleges and presents a preview of the book *College Pathways to the Science Education Standards,* published by the National Science Teachers Association.

The curriculum for courses populated by nonscience majors is often routine and bland. *Designing Nonmajors' Science Courses—Is There a Better Way?* presents a different approach to developing science courses for nonscience majors. Instead of making an effort to show the uniqueness of the scientific way of knowing, the author describes how efforts were made to emphasize the similarities between science and nonscience disciplines.

Two-year colleges should offer a variety of science courses aimed primarily at the nonscientists who form the majority of student populations. *Designing Science Literacy Courses* recommends two key methodological ingredients and two key content-oriented ingredients for a successful liberal-arts science course.

Two-year colleges are committed to meeting community needs. The article *Teaching to Learn: Why Should Teachers Have All the Fun?* describes a natural science class that performed a science-learning activity that went well beyond the usual campus boundaries. The authors describe an advanced teaching technique that involves collaborating with a middle school teacher and a community organization.

Teaching adults is different from working with younger people. Two-year colleges have a higher proportion of these so-called nontraditional students than do four-year colleges and universities. Often the curriculum and teaching approach need to be different for these students. *A Practical Application of Andragogical Theory Assumptions in Introductory Biology Courses* describes how teaching strategies must be altered for the adult learner. The author introduces the term *andragogy* and compares it to *pedagogy.* It is a useful piece for those working with nontraditional students.

Sometimes new curricular approaches in science for nonscience majors raise questions among colleagues and students alike. *A Path Toward Integrated Sciences—The First Steps* examines the design and implementation of an integrated science course for nonscience majors, organized by an interdisciplinary team of instructors, at one community college. The article presents a review of the objectives, problems, criticism, and the growing pains that occur when attempting to create a non-traditional new course.

## Teaching strategies for the two-year college

In addition to curricular issues, science faculty at two-year colleges are concerned with effective teaching strategies. In *Are We Cultivating 'Couch Potatoes' in Our College Science Lectures?* the author recounts an invitation to sit in on a colleague's large biology class at another institution. He describes what he observed and how he was unable to admit to his colleague that the students didn't pay much attention during the lecture and probably didn't learn a great deal. The article reflects on the lecture method and the reluctance of science professors to give up that method and to try other approaches in their classes.

Problems often arise as two-year college teachers move from traditional methods toward innovative ones. *Chaos and Opportunity: Minimizing Obstacles Along the Track to the Constructivist Approach* describes real classroom experiences on the part of the author as he tried to minimize the problems of making the transition from teacher-centered to student-centered instruction. The article identifies several categories of obstacles to innovation and focuses on one of them. Students are one of the obstacles and this article talks about ways to help students adapt to nontraditional teaching methods.

Some two-year college professors have instituted new approaches in their courses, giving up the traditional "lecture method." *Getting There from Here* describes how to make the transition from traditional teaching practices to those that are student-centered. The authors discuss two forms of barriers to this transition and present arguments against these barriers. The article concludes with suggestions on how to use the many resources available to faculty members who want to move their classes away from the standard lecture format to a more active learning environment.

Concerned that science students often fail to understand how science is conducted, and how to interpret communications in science, one professor tried a different method to help students move toward comprehension. In *An Experimental Project Approach to Biology*, this professor describes how he replaced the ecology and environmental science exercises in his biology class with a class experiment that required five weeks to conduct and evaluate. His findings indicate that the project approach helps to develop the interdisciplinary skills used in science.

Other two-year science instructors express concern about students experiencing the "doing" of science, and not just the learning of facts, and want to incorporate project approaches into biology courses. One such project is described in *The Antimicrobial Properties of Red Algae,* which describes a research project in which a professor and student collaborated in the screening of macroscopic algae for antimicrobial properties, and the advantages of such collaboration.

One author conducted a research study to answer questions about incorporating long-term inquiry project experience into a freshman biology course. The article, *Inquiry in the Community College Biology Lab,* examines the inquiry project involving research about crickets. The author explored questions about students' reaction to the project and students' ability to design and carry out a collaborative inquiry project. Other questions central to the research project dealt with students' understanding of the scientific process, the nature of science, and the learning of biology concepts. Students reacted favorably regarding this inquiry experience, and the author presents examples of students' written comments as well as a summary and discussion.

Two-year science faculty often express the belief that it is their responsibility to motivate students—future voters (and funding grantors!)—to think about the importance of scientific enterprises to society. In *A Two-Sided Mirror of Science Education,* the author describes students using critical reflection, the process of thinking about one's opinions and biases, to assume the role of the director of the National Science Foundation and rank five hypothetical government-funded science projects according to funding priority. The author provides positive conclusions about this approach to teaching.

Case studies are another effective way of getting students to be actively involved in the learning of science. *LifeLines OnLine—Curriculum and Teaching Strategies for Adult Learners* gives a step-by-step protocol for using case studies in the classroom. *LifeLines OnLine* was the name of the National Science Foundation–funded workshops at Southeastern Missouri State University. The workshops taught the case study method to two-year college teachers over a three-year period. The Web resources for this technique are still available online at *www.bioquest.org/lifelines.*

Other two-year instructors use case studies in their teaching. *Trouble in Paradise—A Case of Speciation* describes a recovery program for a rodent population on the island of St. Kitts in the Caribbean. Students in introductory biology had to read the case study and formulate their own stories incorporating some of the details and data provided, while also drawing on several evolutionary concepts studied in class. Readers can view examples of student papers done for this case study by accessing the website for the National Center for Case Study Teaching in Science, included in the article.

## Using information and communication technologies

Many two-year college instructors incorporate the use of modern information technology into their courses to make the classes more interactive. Others use the technology to offer opportunities for students through distance learning classes. One such example of integrating modern technology into the classroom is presented in *A Computerized Approach to Mastery Learning*. In this article, the author describes a mastery learning approach using computerized quizzes for students.

Distance learning has become quite common in many post-secondary institutions. Instructors often wonder about how successful the learning process can be for students taking courses through distance learning offerings. *Screening Prospective Laboratory Telecourse Students* examines indicators for student success in distance learning (DL) courses. The authors tell how screening students for certain qualities helps improve success in the DL environment. The push for DL courses needs to be tempered by appropriate advisement. This article is about exploring what that advisement ought to be.

Once professor describes the experience of developing and evaluating a distance learning course in *Teaching Introductory Agriculture Courses Through Distance Education Technology at Louisiana State University*. The author explores the mechanics, advantages, and disadvantages of presenting a distance education class to students at a two-year college. The students had no previous formal education in this discipline.

In addition to developing online courses, faculty have to evaluate student performance in the class itself. *Introductory Biology Online—Assessing Outcomes of Two Student Populations* describes one method of online assessment. The author describes how outcomes assessments were conducted with a pretest/posttest design in an online non-majors' biology course that included laboratory and lecture components. Data were compared with those of students at the same two-year college enrolled in the same course with the same instructor on-campus.

## Conclusion

The two-year college science instructors whose articles are presented in this collection explore the different facets of the two-year college setting and what makes it unique. The authors express concerns about this uniqueness, issues in curriculum development, different teaching strategies, and the impact of the increasing use of modern information technology. The insights expressed in these articles were the result of personal experiences and research studies.

Timothy M. Cooney
NSTA College Division Director, 2001–2004
Professor of Earth Science and Science Education
University of Northern Iowa

# Hello! Is Anybody Out There?

M. W. CAPRIO

diting this column ["The Two-Year College"] for the *Journal of College Science Teaching (JCST)* has given me a national perspective on community colleges that would not have been available to me in any other way. The business of gathering manuscripts and helping the authors prune and shape them to fit the space and objectives of *JCST* has given me a window on the world of two-year schools few other community college teachers enjoy. I have managed to learn a great deal about the rich diversity of these schools and also discovered some of their common characteristics. This column is about one of those commonalities: *isolation*.

The reasons for isolation may be geographical, financial, social, or political—and more likely be a combination of these—but its causes are not the real subject here. The fact is that, in general, two-year schools tend to be somewhat isolated from one another and that may not always be in their best interest. To a point, some isolation may be inevitable because the needs of the service areas of these institutions are frequently highly specialized and are a primary focus (some would say a black hole) for their human and material resources.

There are gains for being so sharply focused. Concentrating the available energy where it is most needed appears, at least in the short run, to be most effective. However, although educators and educational institutions are of the present, they really exist for the future. The impact we have as teachers of young adults is not fully realized in one, two, or even 10 years, and despite the recent cries for accountability—mostly from people who know little about learning, less about teaching, and who usually need results to point to before the next election—teachers do not think in terms of quarterly profits.

When I look at my own academic growth since college I want to reach back to those high school and undergraduate instructors who did so much to shape me into the teacher—and, to a large extent—the person I have become. I would very much like to thank them, but most of them are long dead. Some of the seeds they planted are still sprouting now, while I am contemplating my retirement. So, where do we draw the bottom line to count the profits and losses? Shortsightedness has no place in this business.

The nature of our work requires we take a longer and broader view of what we do, and it seems that the degree to which our myopia increases, the more we manage to isolate ourselves from one another. This is so, I think, partly because each institution has produced a significant body of educational knowledge that could help to plot the future trajectories of other schools. Each undertakes innovative enterprises from time to time and keeps records—if only anecdotally—of outcomes; there are enrollment figures reflecting which promotional strategies worked and which did not; and efforts made to improve retention are documented, for institutional records or to satisfy the requirements of one granting agency or another.

Every school has an enormous data bank that is the outcome of what we call *institutional research* and which we truly believe is of value only to ourselves. We work in isolation on problems that yield information that may well serve the common good, but we do not often share what we learn—community colleges are woefully under-represented in professional education journals and as presenters at conferences. And schools that do not step back for the grander view to see what is out there upon which they can build are doomed to remain mired in the minutia of solving problems for which solutions already exist.

This is not a trivial matter. Educators and educational institutions are, in my view, more than merely *for* the future. They play a major role—perhaps *the* major role—in *creating* that future. This is an enormous responsibility that impacts millions of people, and we need to be as clever and creative as we can if we are to do it right. Teachers in two-year colleges—based on the numbers of students we see—shoulder about half this burden. But only half. If we remain locked in a senseless, busy-work present, our visions will grow stale in a future that will not wait for those who cannot learn from others.

Unlike corporate research, there is no profit motive here for sequestering data and conclusions from the community-at-large. Rather, educational institutions probably only rarely consider what they have learned about their own campuses to be of any more than local interest. And

the other side of the same coin suggests we might also not be likely to seek solutions to problems of our own campuses in databases compiled by others. Celebrating diversity too enthusiastically may be a kind of hubris that leads to blindness about what we actually do have in common.

Chief among the losses isolation brings are the inevitable redundancies it spawns. For no matter how specialized local needs may be, it is difficult to imagine that there is no other educational institution somewhere that has not already wrestled with—and solved—precisely the same problem or some analog of it. Where resources are limited, isolation may represent hidden operational costs, which may be considerable and which are usually extravagant. Building atop the work of others promises an easier climb and would surely bring the climbers to even greater heights. But scientists have known that for centuries.

Considering the usual readership of this column, it is probably safe to say that, while all of us are clever and creative, none of us is as clever and as creative as we can be when we work together. And reinvention is clearly not one of the more clever things we do. If the cost of rediscovery and reduplicating work is a price we pay for our isolation, it follows that reducing this overhead will lead to greater efficiency in the form of more rapid growth, conserved resources, and recaptured time, all of which can yield dividends when invested elsewhere. R&D may be alive and well at two-year colleges, but if we can improve our connectivity to one another, the future we are creating for our institutions, our students, and beyond will carry a much lower price tag.

## Now what?

How can community colleges better link with one another for their mutual benefit? Most—maybe all—answers to this question carry some costs. Of course, a big part of what makes any program affordable has to do with the value we perceive it to have for us and the priority we choose to assign to it. There are many other possibilities, but consider: hosting regional and state two-year college science conferences; promoting cross-pollination by underwriting programs to exchange faculty between different two-year schools or between two-year schools and universities; obtaining memberships in national professional societies and providing realistic support (*realistic* is a key concept here) for faculty to attend their conventions; and temporarily freeing interested individuals from part of the very heavy teaching load most two-year college teachers have so they can do institutional, educational, and discipline-based research *and* write about it for the professional journals *and* present their work at professional meetings. The expenditures these entail are really investments that reduce redundancies and promote institutional growth.

## And then there's the Internet

Attending conferences may not always be possible, but accessing the Internet is becoming increasingly facile because two-year schools across the country are installing the requisite technology and getting on line. The Net is an immense resource, but it immediately poses several questions. The first, and the only one I have space to at least partially address here is: How can community colleges and, more specifically, community college science teachers find one another out there, in cyberspace?

The two most popular things to look for are webpages and listservs. Individuals have their own pages on the World Wide Web (WWW) and so do many community colleges. It is probably easier and more productive to search for institutional webpages first. You can obtain a list of community colleges with a Web presence and the address of each website from a WWW page maintained by the Maricopa Community College District. The URL is:

*www.mcli.dist.maricopa.edu/cc/search.html*

At this writing it listed over 1,200 two-year colleges in the United States, Canada, and Europe and allowed the visitor to search by geographic region and, for schools in the United States, by state. Each of the schools listed at this site has a webpage, and clicking on the name of the college transports you to its WWW address.

The University of Texas at Austin maintains a similar list. You can jump to it from a link on the Maricopa page or can go directly to:

*www.utexas.edu/world/comcol/alpha/*

I found 804 U.S. community colleges listed there, and it allowed searching alphabetically or by state. Unlike the Maricopa list, not all the schools listed here are active on the Web, but the ones that have webpages are color coded and you can click on their names and easily jump to their homepages.

When a cyberspace traveler arrives at a homepage there are options to move to related pages. Many schools will have links to their academic departments' pages, campus telephone directories, their college bulletins, and various special projects that are under way, to mention just a few of the more common options.

Once you reach a college's homepage, finding your counterpart at the other school is a simple matter. A short note will quickly let you know if you have someone who can supply the sort of information you need, or if they will be able to direct you to someone on their campus who can. Correspondence begun this way can produce only the desired information exchange. However, it can also result in collaborative projects that may lead to joint presentations at conferences, the formation of articulation agreements between institutions, and sharing of resources. The first step is to talk to one another. Another way of connecting with others who have common interests is to search for mailing lists, also called listservs. Members of mailing lists e-mail their messages to a server, a specialized computer, which sends the message out to all the other members, who then can respond to the original message. The result is an ongoing dialog on specific topics with other people having common interests.

A way to locate mailing lists is to point your Web browser at the following URL:

*www.tile.net/lists*

This website is a searchable list of mailing lists. You can do keyword searches to find topics of interest. For most entries, the search returns the name of the list; its country of origin; where it is located; an e-mail address for the computer administrator, to whom you will send your commands to subscribe or to unsubscribe, for example; an e-mail address for the human administrator, who will answer your questions; and directions of how to subscribe. Here are a few examples of the output of this website.

MODELING
Physics Modeling Workshop
Country: USA
Site: University of Illinois at Chicago, Chicago, IL, USA
Computerized Administrator: listserv@listserv.uic.edu
Human administrator: modeling-request@listserv.uic.edu
You can join this group by sending the message "sub MODELING your name" to listserv@listserv.uic.edu

L-ACLRNG
Active and Collaborative Learning
Country: USA
Site: Pennsylvania State University
Computerized Administrator: listserv@psuvm.psu.edu
Human administrator: l-aclrng-request@psuvm.psu.edu
You can join this group by sending the message "sub L-ACLRNG your name" to listserv@psuvm.psu.edu

NCPRSE-L
Reform Discussion List for Science Education
Country: USA

Site: East Carolina University, Computing and Info Systems, Greenville, North Carolina
Computerized Administrator: listserv@ecuvm.cis.ecu.edu
Human administrator: ncprse-l-request@ecuvm.cis.ecu.edu
You can join this group by sending the message "sub NCPRSE-L your name" to listserv@ecuvm.ecu.cis.edu

COMMCOLL
No title defined [discussion of community college issues]
Country: USA
Site: None given [University of Kentucky Community College System]
Computerized Administrator: listserv@lsv.uky.edu
Human administrator: commcoll-request@lsv.uky.edu
You can join this group by sending the message "sub COMMCOLL your name" to listserv@lsv.uky.edu

Once you get the information about the lists of interest, you might want to write to the human administrators to verify the kinds of posts that are appropriate for them before you subscribe. The listserv (computer administrator) will verify your subscription and send you instructions for communicating with the list as well as the commands you will need to "speak" with it to control mail flow. Be sure to download those instructions and save them for future reference.

Mailing lists can take us well beyond our campus boundaries to interact with colleagues across the country and even around the world without ever getting on an airplane. And, they are fun.

# The First Day of Class on a Two-Year Campus

*What Students Really Want Us to Know about Their Science Classroom Experiences*

M.M. COWAN AND K.W. PIEPGRASS

During the course of a three-year study of science attitudes among nonscience majors at two, two-year regional campuses of Miami University (Ohio), we found our ideas about student anxiety did not always coincide with the reality painted for us by the students.

While some of the anxiety-provoking factors identified by the students in the study were expected and have already been documented in literature (e.g., lack of preparedness, unfamiliar vocabulary), one issue that was repeatedly "penciled-in" by the students, since we did not address it on our surveys or in our interviews, was the first day of class. Students reported that this earliest experience plays a very important role in determining the level of anxiety in physics, microbiology, and chemistry

> *I know not anything more pleasant, or more instructive, than to compare experience with expectation, or to register from time to time the difference between idea and reality.*
>
> *—SAMUEL JOHNSON, 1758*

courses. Once again, here is an example of the students teaching the teachers.

Our study distinguished between two types of nonmajors: the science-related nonmajor (SR), who is often enrolled in allied health degree programs such as nursing or physical therapy, and the general studies student (GS), who majors in an unrelated field and takes science courses to fulfill the university's liberal education requirements.

The academic profile of the student body at these Miami University branch campuses reflects the trend in higher education toward "nontraditional" students: Many have returned to school after an absence of some years (59 percent were 22 years of age or more), many reported having poor (or no) science preparation, a significant number were considered "at-risk" students, and many had multiple job/family/home responsibilities in addition to their school demands.

## Anxiety and the two-year student

In our study, 12 percent of 436 respondents reported high to very high anxiety about their science courses at the beginning of the semester (Cowan and Piepgrass, 1997). To determine the causes of this angst, we convened focus groups consisting of volunteers from six introductory courses (three GS and three SR courses) in three departments early in the semester. Students were solicited with the promise of pizza and the chance to comment on their science courses.

The students themselves determined the format of the early focus group meetings. The leader simply stated that members of the science faculty wanted to hear from students about the environment in science courses at this campus and whether they felt any anxiety. Later sessions sometimes included a handout with three questions typed on a sheet of paper that was used to spark discussion (e.g., Do you feel anxiety? What causes the anxiety? How could the course/instructor reduce anxiety?). Someone other than the course instructor conducted the focus groups, with the promise of anonymity, and we informed participants that the session was not meant to be a "gripe session" about particular instructors.

Invariably, each group contained a minority of students who reported no anxiety. However, the students who did report anxiety were eager to name its causes. During these sessions and on open-ended questionnaires administered in class, clear differences emerged on the reported origins of anxiety among science-related nonmajors and general studies nonmajors, although both types of students volunteered that first-day issues (which were not mentioned by the group leader or on the questionnaires) were uppermost on their list as a cause or a source of relief from science anxiety. This unexpected outcome was made more compelling because it was brought up in every session by one or more students, and once it was mentioned, most individuals expressed strong feelings about it.

Science teachers at two-year colleges know that anxiety in the classroom can be palpable in the initial days of a semester. There are good reasons for student uneasiness to appear early, although it may have less to do with a student's degree of self-confidence than a lack of framework of prior knowledge (Anderson and Clawson, 1992). Anxiety is also aggravated by students' perceived loss of personal control. Perceived personal control is linked to factors such as depression, crowding, marital relations, academic achievement, health, aging, and stress (Perry, 1991). On two-year campuses such as those of Miami University, students are likely to have both a weaker framework of prior knowledge and problems in one or more of the areas linked to perceived personal control. Indeed, two-year campuses often experience high levels of science attrition as well as student fear and dissatisfaction associated with science courses.

Researchers have also well documented the effects of anxiety on student performance (reviewed in Hembree, 1988). We discovered in our study that anxiety was negatively correlated with first exam scores among GS students (Cowan and Piepgrass, 1997).

Low levels of perceived personal control may be stable or transient, and thus can be influenced by the teacher and other environmental factors (Perry, 1991). Studies have shown that the classroom context and manner in which courses are packaged by faculty could evoke more positive attitudes in students (Everson, 1994; Okebukola, 1986). The surveyed students agreed that the first day of class was an important part of that packaging.

Our study found that the anxiety reported by the two types of nonmajors had different sources (Table 1). Data in Table 1 represent answers to the open-ended, first-day survey question, "What, if anything, makes you feel anxious about this class?" Not unexpectedly, GS students found the subject itself anxiety provoking. Science-related majors, however, stated that anxiety was triggered less often by the subject than

**Table 1.**

Source of Anxiety for Nonmajors (adapted from Cowan and Piepgrass, in review)

|  | General Studies n=194 | Related Majors n=242 |
|---|---|---|
| **Subject Specific** top 3 responses | 50% last science not recent "I'm bad in science" hard topic | 42% hard topic last science not recent "I'm bad in science" |
| **Other** top 3 responses | 14% need a good grade test anxiety unprepared | 35% hearsay need good grade returning student |

**Table 2.**

First Day of Class Strategies

- Keep students the whole period, but don't give any "testable" material.

- Give them an informal introduction to your discipline (slide show, newspaper articles).

- Teach specific science-reading skills.

- Hand out a non-intimidating yet complete syllabus.

- Be clear about course expectations and procedures while providing flexibility for SR students.

- Remind students how much they already know by giving pre-tests geared towards everyday scientific knowledge and asking for personal essays about infections, kitchen chemistry, etc.

- Put your course in a context that's meaningful to students; Bring in a tape from TV, such as *20/20* or *The X Files* that uses concepts from your discipline.

- Tell your own story of some struggle you had with science sometime in your academic career.

- Tell a story of your success! (Students like to hear about instructors' experiences.)

for the general studies students. SR students reported more of what could be called general anxiety (e.g., "I'm a returning student," "I've heard this is hard"). The latter comment, which we call hearsay, is one science instructors hear constantly (Schwartz, et al., 1985). We believe it is a major nonspecific contributor to anxiety—and one that can be addressed on the first day.

## How the first day can help—and hurt

The aspect of the first day of class mentioned most often and in equal numbers by both GS and SR students as causing anxiety surprisingly involved not starting lecture from the first meeting. Here's a hot button! Ask a dozen instructors and you will get a dozen different opinions, usually strong ones, about lecturing immediately. Many feel that the "tyranny of content" demands that lecture begin in that first hour. Others feel that it sets the tone for the course, initiating a culture of rigor. Of course it does set the tone, but if the tone is interpreted as hostile, foreign, or intimidating it may have major implications for student success. In one case, a professor who distributed a lengthy syllabus on the first day of class found that information overload and disenfranchisement of the students occurred (Smith and Razzouk, 1993). Diving in on the first day could result in similar student responses, though there is little data about first-day behavior in literature. Interested readers should refer to a study by Wieneke (1981), a commentary by Dorn (1987), and proceedings from a symposium on the topic (Schwartz et al., 1985) for more information.

The GS students offered the following first-day suggestions for easing student fears: make the syllabus specific and full of dates and details about the course management, and do something exciting! We should infer from this last suggestion that students will need their imaginations sparked before they can be motivated to succeed in an unfamiliar field. In fact, a meta-analysis of attitude and achievement among elementary and college-age students found that interest was at least as closely correlated with achievement as attitude (i.e., anxiety) (Willson, 1983). The request for detail on the syllabus may suggest that students feel little desire for autonomy with a subject that is foreign to them. Two of the three focus groups also did not want instructors to act in a condescending manner toward them. Although "being babied" did not contribute to their anxiety, they stated that it did decrease their investment in the course.

In contrast, science-related majors were more interested in having a voice in the management and content of the course, suggesting that some room for negotiation be left on the syllabus. These students also asked for explicit training in how to learn science, how to read the text, etc. Finally, they identified instructor organization as important, saying they "felt nervous about the amount of material" required in a class. However, seeing that the instructor had planned ahead and ordered the information into manageable chunks put them at ease.

In summary, our focus group participants pleaded for a different approach to the first day of class. Those who had a science-related major were most anxious about general issues and sug-

gested that instructors spend the first day soliciting student input about course content and management and specifically in explaining how to learn the subject matter. General studies students had more subject-specific anxieties and sought additional structure as well as some convincing that the material would be worth their time. Both groups asked for time to acclimate themselves to the course. Table 2 summarizes possible first-day strategies suggested by the students themselves and by researchers who have identified methods that address the specific sources cited by our study population. If it is, indeed, necessary to recognize emotional as well as cognitive obstacles to learning (Mallow and Greenburg, 1983), understanding these self-reported student barriers from the first day of class should help us to assist students to uncover their own capacity to learn.

## References

Anderson, G.A., and K. Clawson. 1992. Science Anxiety in Our Colleges: Origins, Implications and Cures. *The Education Resources Information Center, ED 354 813:1-28.*

Cowan, M.M., and K.W. Piepgrass. 1997. Attitudes about science among non-majors at a two-year campus of a liberal arts university. ERIC document 411 034

Dorn, D.S. 1987. The first day of class: Problems and strategies. *Teaching Sociology* 15:61-72.

Everson, H.T., S. Tobias, H. Hartman, and A. Gourgey. 1994. Test Anxiety and the Curriculum: The Subject Matters. The Education Resources Information Center, ED 366 598:1-19.

Hembree, R. 1988. Correlates, causes, effects, and treatment of test anxiety. *Review of Educational Research* 58:47-77.

Mallow, J.V., and S.L. Greenburg. 1983. Science anxiety and science learning. *The Physics Teacher* 21:95-99.

Okebukola, P.A. 1986. Reducing anxiety in science classes: An experiment involving some models of class interaction. *Educational Research* 28:146-149.

Perry, R.P. 1991. Perceived control in college students: Implications for instruction in higher education. In *Higher Education: Handbook of Theory and Research,* pp. 1-56. New York: Agathon Press.

Schwartz, A.T., C. Schrader, K. Dombrink, B.G. Smith, H.A. Bent, and D.W. Brooks. 1985. The first day of class—A DIVCHED symposium. *Journal of Chemical Education* 62:601-605.

Smith, M.F., and N.Y. Razzouk. 1993. Improving classroom communication: The case of the course syllabus. *Journal of Education for Business* 68:215-221.

Wieneke, C. 1981. The first lecture: Implications for students who are new to the university. *Studies in Higher Education* 6:85-89.

Willson, V.L. 1983. A meta-analysis of the relationship between science achievement and science attitude: Kindergarten through college. *Journal of Research in Science Teaching* 20:839-850.

# Adjunct Faculty

## A Multidimensional Perspective on the Important Work of Part-time Faculty

M. W. CAPRIO, NATHAN DUBOWSKY, ROBERT L. WARASILA,
DIANE D. CHEATWOOD, AND FRANCES T. COSTA

*djunct faculty*, also known as *associate* or *part-time faculty*, have been steadily growing in proportion to full-time staff in all types of postsecondary institutions. But overall, the two-year schools have clearly outpaced the four-year colleges and universities in this staffing area.

Data from the National Center for Educational Statistics (1993) reveal 40 percent of all college faculty are part-time teachers. At community colleges, however, the adjunct faculty comprise 64 percent of the classroom teachers. There are two important reasons for the large numbers of adjuncts at the two-year schools. These colleges do not rely on graduate teaching assistants as do four-year colleges and universities. Indeed, in 1993, graduate teaching assistants exceeded the number of full-timers at those institutions. Secondly, it is primarily the two-year schools that tailor their offerings to meet the needs of nontraditional students by offering, for example, classes on weekends and in the evenings on main campuses and at remote sites. Traditional teaching schedules typical of full-time instructors do not easily accommodate the needs of such a diverse instructional delivery system, and part-time instructors fill the gaps.

The popular wisdom about adjunct faculty is that they pose a risk of diminished instructional quality in the classroom. This concern, however, is not supported by the literature. Studies that rely on student evaluations of part-time teachers typically show no difference between the two types of teachers (Cruise, Furst, and Klimes, 1980; Behrendt and Parsons, 1983).

But students may not be the best judge of teachers. Comparisons of teaching effectiveness by means of pre- and posttests administered to students in the same courses taught by teachers in both employment categories revealed no significant difference in student performance outcomes (Kamps, 1998). And a study of grade distributions by Stovall (1994) found that, "...the amount of variation within each group...is greater than the variation between all full-time faculty compared to all part-time faculty teaching the same class in a given term."

The real disadvantages of having "too many" adjunct faculty may be attributable to factors other than those related to what they do in their classrooms. One concern is that because adjuncts work for proportionally less pay than full-timers, their presence helps to keep down full-time salaries and reduce the probability of recruiting the best available faculty for tenure-track positions. Then, too, because the part-time faculty is usually not compensated for working with students outside of class, nontraditional students—who usually need more out-of-class support—may find themselves at a disadvantage with an adjunct instructor. Finally, part-time faculty rarely serve on campus committees, they provide little, if any, input to campus governance issues, and they do not usually contribute to curriculum development. Thus, as the part-time staff grows, there are proportionally fewer full-timers to carry out these and other collegial activities, which ultimately weakens the instructional quality of the institution and the coherence of its programs.

On the other hand, adjunct instructors offer some important advantages. They fill those time slots without which many students would be denied courses at a time and place where they can attend them. They bring affordable, specialized expertise to small schools that would be unable to hire full-time specialists in certain disciplines. And adjuncts are cost efficient, which can make programs possible that might otherwise not be economically feasible.

## The purpose of this paper

In order to provide a multidimensional perspective on adjunct faculty, I have invited four contributors to this column.

• *Nathan Dubowsky* is a full-time community college instructor who has served as an adjunct at a major university, a four-year state college, and at community colleges other than his home institution.

• *Robert Warasila* is a physical science department administrator. I have asked him to write about adjunct faculty from that perspective.

• *Diane Cheatwood* is a professional development officer at a community college that uses more than the average number of adjunct faculty and manages them through a comprehensive professional development program that she will describe briefly.

• Finally, *Frances Costa,* who—at this writing—was a full-time biomedical researcher working as an adjunct instructor at two community col-

leges, will offer some insights about how adjunct instructors can be better utilized.

I think it is interesting to note the differences as well as the similarities in their points of view.

## Facilitating the adjunct role

### Nathan Dubowsky

Each semester, hundreds of thousands of adjunct instructors enter college classrooms to teach virtually every course offered at the collegiate level. Those who teach in adjunct positions do so for a wide variety of reasons: some are recent graduates who are "auditioning" for full-time positions; others are piecing together a livelihood by teaching courses at several different schools; there are those who, while actively employed in research or industry, welcome the opportunity to return to the classroom where they can share their knowledge with those who will soon enter their fields; and there are even experienced full-time instructors who enjoy the additional challenge of teaching a different course at a different school.

Much has been written about the advantages of employing adjuncts as ways to cope with fluctuations in enrollment, maintain flexible scheduling, and reduce the financial commitment of tenure. Far less has been written about the ways that colleges and universities can optimize the status and conditions under which adjuncts work. It is the purpose of this discussion to examine one person's experiences as an adjunct and to provide some suggestions for what academic institutions can do to facilitate the effectiveness of its adjunct faculties for the benefit of the students, the colleges, and the adjuncts themselves. For several years, I have served as an adjunct professor teaching evolution in both the upper division of a state-supported four-year college and at a graduate school of a major university. As a full-time teacher at a community college, I enjoy the academic challenge of teaching a specialized course and the prestige of being a member of the faculty of a graduate school. I also serve as an informal and unofficial mentor and resource person for several adjunct instructors teaching in the biology department at my community college.

In this capacity, I listen as my adjunct faculty colleagues recount their successes and failures in the classroom as well as their frustrations, confusions, and feelings of isolation as they attempt to navigate the unique features of our department and college. Answers to questions as simple as "How do I get paid?" or " Am I expected to type and duplicate my own syllabi and examinations?" can become sources of consternation to those unfamiliar with the system. These experiences, collected over time, as well as my own experiences as an adjunct faculty member, have taught me how difficult and confusing it can be to be a part-time instructor. And, it has also shown me that many of the difficulties adjuncts face can be anticipated and eliminated if there is a carefully crafted, formalized support system in place.

Although many adjuncts are seasoned professionals with years of teaching experience, it is a mistake to assume that they will know all that is expected of them at a particular institution and how they can effectively satisfy these expectations. Therefore, a reasonable starting point in the creation of a structured support system would be the creation of an official handbook specifically designed for adjuncts. Written by the college administration, with supplementary information provided by the department in which the person is teaching, this handbook should contain, at the very least, the following:

• *clear and unambiguous statements of what the college and the department expect of its part-time teachers (i.e., the policies, rules, regulations, and responsibilities);*
• *the answers to practical questions most full-time faculty consider so "obvious" that they do not think it necessary to convey to adjuncts new to the college and the department. (e.g., What am I expected to do in a specific emergency situation? How do I get examinations typed and duplicated? Where and how do I get*

*chalk to write on the blackboard? How and where do I get a key to the...? How do I contact laboratory support personnel to request a specific laboratory setup?) This section would be of particular importance to adjunct faculty who teach at unusual times or at remote locations where there may be no full-time colleagues to consult;*
• *a list of the support persons they may need to contact when special circumstance arise (campus security, medical and psychological services, immediate supervisors, etc.).*

However, no written document can substitute for interpersonal relationships. Although some full-time faculty do take it upon themselves to establish and maintain working relationships with adjunct faculty, and some adjunct faculty do seek out and establish relationships with their full-time colleagues, these kinds of interactions should not be left to happenstance. Instead we should formalize bridges for communication. We could do this by officially designating one or more full-time faculty who have experience serving as adjuncts and who are sensitive to the needs of adjunct faculty to serve as *Adjunct Faculty Mentors*. These individuals would have the responsibility of working with, assisting, and advising adjuncts.

In most cases, adjuncts would like to be part of the college and departmental community, and would be, given the chance. They often have much that they can and would like to contribute to the academic community. It would be the role of the Adjunct Faculty Mentors to encourage and facilitate the inclusion of adjunct faculty in the activities of the department and the college as a whole.

Despite all pronouncements to the contrary, adjunct faculty are here to stay. For this reason alone, we must invite them to join in, and welcome them as valued partners in the teaching community. We need to maximize their effectiveness and their input to the teaching and learning community of which they are such an integral part. While no one individual can provide all of the answers as to how this can and should be done, the time is right for a dialogue on these issues.

## A department head's perspective

*Robert L. Warasila*

The physical sciences department at Suffolk County Community College (SCCC) in Selden, New York, offers courses in physics, chemistry, and the Earth and space sciences. The department's administration includes a department head and two assistant department heads, with each administrator having responsibility for one of the three disciplines. We each have five hours of administrative release time and 10 hours of classroom teaching time. The college bases a portion of the release time formula on the number of hours taught by adjunct faculty, ostensibly to provide us with time to oversee their academic assignments.

Our institution is a multi-campus facility with 60 percent of the students attending the main campus. SCCC encourages the full-time staff to teach overload courses allowing up to five contact hours in the day session in addition to the regular teaching load. Each physical sciences department administrator generally elects to teach five hours of overload. Even so, it is necessary, especially for the evening program, to expand the instructional staff by using part-time instructors. This has become more necessary as the faculty has advanced in age and affluence and has opted for fewer overload assignments. The percentage of hours taught by adjuncts varies widely among departments, but in the physical sciences we have worked hard to keep the total adjunct-taught hours at 40 percent or less.

Most of the adjuncts currently enrolled in our department have been with us for 15 to 20 years. They bring a variety of backgrounds to the classroom including that of high school teachers; full-time, upper-division college teachers; engineers, programmers, research scientists at public and corporate laboratories; and entrepreneurs. Clearly, the diversity of disciplines and expertise infuses rich educational and workplace experience into our department.

Although we have done little to promote interactions of adjuncts with the full-time staff in a formal way, we have actively encouraged informal exchanges with our adjuncts on topics ranging from what the high schools are currently like to what industry and upper-level colleges expect of our graduates. These exchanges usually take place during the time before classes meet when we are passing in the halls. This is perhaps the greatest value of the adjunct presence in our department. They bring to us valuable information about what is happening in the community beyond our campus.

In addition to their isolation from full-time colleagues in their discipline, adjuncts are even less likely to interact with faculty outside their subject area.

I believe this is because they are pressed for time and cannot participate in the collegial activities and campus governance required of the full-time staff and which forces full-time faculty of different disciplines to share ideas about the institution.

There is a teacher's union at our college, and adjunct faculty work under the same bargaining unit and contract as full-time staff. The contract does, however, provide full-time instructors preference in course choice, even their overload. I have found adjunct participation in the bargaining unit to be disappointing, probably because for most this is not their primary employment. They appear to choose to not actively participate in the faculty union or in college governance bodies. The irony is that, as a group, the adjunct faculty have enough votes (half a vote each) to control the bargaining group.

After full-time faculty have made their choices, we base adjunct course assignments on seniority (semesters taught). We usually try to build adjunct availability into the department schedule so that there are few surprises when the staffing process is complete. Course offerings frequently are dictated by the availability of suitable adjuncts. Our department has strong academic principles regarding adjunct assignment;

the Office of Instruction rules require a master's degree in the discipline being taught, and our department achieves that goal with few exceptions.

The college applies a variety of policies to make adjuncts feel they are part of the institution. At the beginning of each semester, the Office of Instruction hosts a reception/meeting for all adjuncts to announce promotions and awards for the adjunct staff. These events are generally attended by about a quarter of the adjunct faculty members and a majority of the department administrators.

At the department level, we make sure all adjuncts are contacted early in the schedule development process to ensure that all our courses can be staffed and that we can come as close to satisfying as many adjunct teaching preferences as possible.

We also involve adjuncts in the textbook selection process, but we usually do not allow individual adoptions in multi-section courses; for most courses, full-timers and adjuncts accept the consensus choice of a text. In cases where only one section of a course is being offered, we usually allow the adjunct to choose the materials. Common course outlines are the norm, although individual diversity is encouraged in matters such as test schedules, questions, and so forth.

Although there are many positive aspects of the adjunct presence, there are also difficulties. The principal problem is accessibility. At SCCC most adjuncts do not have reserved office space. As offices become available we try to allocate one or more for adjuncts to share. In some cases where personalities fit, a full-timer will invite an adjunct to share space in his or her office. But office space remains as a major problem. Without a permanent location, it is difficult for adjuncts to set up office hours if they wish to. Adjuncts are not required to provide office hours, but we encourage them to budget time before and after class to meet with students, although we have no enforcement power.

Another major problem stems from our multi-campus organization and contractual se-

niority rights. Adjuncts can be brought onto the seniority list from any of three campuses. In an effort to exercise some uniformity of standards the Office of Instruction holds a meeting at the end of the spring semester with department administrators from each campus to certify new adjuncts. Unfortunately only the campus that has worked with the individual is privy to any shortcomings.

Attendance problems sometimes arise with adjuncts because of travel obligations associated with their full-time jobs. This is especially true of adjuncts who are engineers or R&D people. Ordinarily this means one of our full-timers will have to stand in so as not to lose precious class time.

Matching adjuncts to an appropriate course can be difficult. We have some adjuncts who can effectively teach courses at all levels, but we also have some who are only effective in particular classes.

In the Earth and space science area we have an abundance of retired high school teachers available as adjuncts. One must be very careful with these candidates: Many are excellent and demanding classroom instructors, but others still hold the "pass them along" philosophy reinforced by their previous career. In addition, some of these teachers are the same people who failed to stimulate our students years before in the local high schools. How can we expect any more from them now that they are teaching in the community college?

Lastly there sometimes arises a kind of loyalty problem. A few of our adjuncts belong to that unfortunate group of college educators who have no full-time position anywhere. These poor souls make a living by working for adjunct pay rates at two or more institutions. They are, very often, awaiting the appearance of a full-time line. Generally they work very hard, even volunteering to participate in collegial activities, such as club advisement and authoring curriculum materials. These are the best of the adjuncts in that regard, and they are effectively serving a kind of apprenticeship for the full-time appointment they hope to achieve.

A dilemma occurs for us when a full-time position does become available. In light of the presence of these more highly committed adjuncts, how can we maintain our objectivity in reviewing all applicants?

How would we change the adjunct environment in our department? First, we would like to hold meetings periodically (twice/semester?) to discuss their impressions of our educational process vis-à-vis their "outside" experiences. We would like to see every adjunct once a week just to say hello. We'd like to have more flexibility with use of adjuncts independent of their position on the seniority list.

Finally, I'd like to be able to retire a few adjuncts! But in the end, I fully understand and appreciate that without adjunct faculty members our institution would be in very serious trouble.

## Different titles, similar needs

### Diane Cheatwood

Usually hired as content experts, not education experts, part-time faculty have many of the same needs and concerns as their full-time colleagues. They want to be effective teachers and see their students learn and succeed both personally and professionally. Because they recognize there are many types of learners in their classes, they want to meet the needs of these diverse students. And, adjunct instructors often have experience in business and industry, so they value the skills they know students will need in the future as highly as the information and knowledge students receive from their classes.

Because many adjunct instructors don't have education backgrounds, they often fall back on their own student experiences of innumerable hours of lecture, punctuated only by a mid-term and final exam, with little formative feedback on student progress. They may experiment on their own with innovative learning techniques only to meet with enormous student resistance. And, in addition, many new instructors need guidance with classroom management, student-centered

learning activities, and ways to become more relaxed in the classroom. They need help, both formal and informal, with the everyday problems and concerns of teaching.

The Community College of Aurora (CCA) in Aurora, Colorado, is a teaching and learning institution with the instructional philosophy that *telling is not teaching*. With 5,500 students and 2,400 FTEs (full-time equivalents), we have about 30 full-time and 270 part-time instructors. With this unusual arrangement, CCA graduates who transfer to four-year institutions have grade point averages that are usually higher than the native students of those institutions. Our faculty development program for full- and part-time instructors includes offerings to help teachers help students to succeed.

*New Faculty Orientation* (NFO) gives new instructors an opportunity to experience active learning and student-centered classes even before they start teaching at CCA. Because of our student-centered teaching philosophy, we think teaching at CCA is a different experience than it is at many other colleges.

In NFO, we examine profiles of typical CCA students, analyze student needs, and identify classroom techniques and college resources to help meet these needs. We spend time discussing the syllabus, the first class, a semester timeline, Bloom's Taxonomy (Bloom, 1956), and workplace safety. Throughout the day-long session we model cooperative learning techniques that the new instructors can apply directly to their classes. Almost all NFO participants are part-time because almost all full-time positions are filled within the college.

Our *Faculty Mentor Program* was designed by the faculty to meet their needs as new instructors: to orient subject-area experts to the world of classroom teaching and help them begin to change from teacher-centered to student-centered instruction. Mentors pair with new instructors for one semester to answer questions about college policies and procedures, provide feedback about teaching performance through two classroom observations, suggest instructional methods and materials, and assist new instructors with other classroom-related concerns.

Potential mentors are identified by division chairs and attend a three-hour workshop in which we (1) define *mentor* at CCA; (2) discuss mentor responsibilities; (3) practice observations and feedback; and (4) address sensitive situations. Both full-time and part-time instructors mentor at CCA; part-time faculty receive an additional contract to mentor a new instructor for one semester.

*Mid-Semester Problem Solving* (MSPS) is a three-hour session to which participants bring their questions and concerns. We use a problem-solving method (Chaffee, 1997) in a practice situation that highlights basic classroom management problems. Then groups solve each other's written problems, discuss options, and open the session to ideas from the entire group. We also discuss how this problem-solving technique could be applied in participants' classes.

*Faculty Development Workshops,* open to all faculty, are a significant part of helping adjuncts realize they are an important part of our teaching institution. Part-time faculty are paid to attend these sessions, as well as the NFO and MSPS. Most of our workshops are four hours long, usually relatively short on theory and long on practice and practical application. We try to walk the talk: we identify objectives, make a personal connection with each participant, provide facts and theory as needed, give both individuals and groups opportunities to discuss and practice, identify ways to use the tool or technique in various disciplines, and always give time to debrief after group and individual reports. This honors the knowledge and experience our faculty brings to the college and provides many more examples and ideas than a lecture would offer.

Our workshops offer both basic topics and sessions designed for more experienced teachers, but they are open to everyone (even a discipline-specific science department workshop is open to all faculty). Facilitated by both part- and full-time CCA faculty, these interdisciplinary sessions offer new ways to view teaching and learning that may be outside the experience of someone who has studied one area exclusively.

Grading and assessment, cooperative learning, improving lectures, student-centered classroom activities, diversity, and syllabus preparation are the basic workshop topics. We offer them on a rotating basis, and we include more specialized session topics as needed, such as learning/teaching styles, ethics, writing and library research, classroom assessment techniques, learners with disabilities, and study skills. We base the schedule on data collected from workshop evaluations, conversations, and an annual faculty survey.

*Year-Long Projects* (YLPs) provide more opportunity for growth and change than anything else we offer in faculty development at CCA. Faculty complete 18–20 hours of workshops on a specific topic the first semester, then implement at least two new ideas in their classes, complete peer coaching, attend additional information sessions, and evaluate the project in a final report during the second semester. We have completed YLPs on thinking skills, ethics, CATs, diversity, study skills, writing across the curriculum, learning styles, and course design. YLPs provide faculty with an opportunity to take risks in the classroom, with a peer coach to advise them while they make improvements they might have considered but rarely had time to study or implement.

Workshops are a cost-effective way to help the part- and full-time faculty become better teachers, but sometimes just a personal conversation or individual consultation can help teachers identify and overcome problems. For example, every person who has tried cooperative-learning activities in class (or least those of us who will admit it) has met with student resistance. Some students who learn best from others eagerly and effectively work in groups. But many of our students have been academically successful by recording the teacher's words and feeding them back verbatim. These individuals need specific reasons why they should put in the extra effort that group work entails.

Clearly explaining the reasons for group work softens resistance and helps students find personal worth in the activity. For example, businesses tell us they need workers who can work effectively in teams, plan projects, self-monitor their work, and evaluate when the project is completed. Meaningful activities give students practice to think, write, and talk like experts in the field. And complex, real-life situations provide opportunity to analyze, synthesize, and evaluate according to the standards of the field.

Faculty who set up activities clearly and logically, stay out of the way during the activity, and then "unpack" both the content and the process, usually find students increase their depth of content knowledge along with their teamwork skills. Concerns about effective teaching, meeting the needs of diverse learners, and handling classroom matters are not exclusive to part-time faculty. Methods to address these topics work equally well with both part- and full-time faculty. A comprehensive faculty development program that addresses not only the technical, but also the affective aspects of teaching, will help avoid the "sink or swim" approach to college instruction. And, combined with the hard work of both students and faculty, will lead to success for all.

## Adjuncts acting as liaisons: The missing link

### *Frances T. Costa and M. W. Caprio*

Adjunct instructors typically teach one or two courses, and usually—often because of commitments to their full-time employment—spend very little time on campus outside of their classrooms. They meet and interact with few of the full-time instructors. Indeed, the only significant professional contact some may have is with the department head, who hands them a course syllabus and a textbook at the beginning of the semester and evaluates their teaching sometime before the term ends. These faculty members seem to be a seriously underutilized resource.

Adjunct science instructors bring many positive attributes with them to the two-year college campus, but not all they have to offer is optimized by the institutions at which they teach. Since adjuncts usually hold full-time professional positions related to the course they teach (but usually not in the field of education), they bring special real-world experience with them when they walk into the classroom. As engineers, research scientists, and medical personnel in their full-time worlds, adjunct instructors have a perspective on teaching not generally available to full-time educators.

My experience (F. Costa) as a full-time research scientist at a major university and as an adjunct instructor of biology at two community colleges is a case in point. Whenever possible, I incorporate my work experience into the cognitive and affective aspects of my teaching. This breathes life into the course and ignites student interest in a way that pure textbook learning cannot. The students are very interested in learning about recent research projects and are very receptive to hearing about my experiences. I find this more personal context to be an effective avenue to the prescribed subject matter. Some students—mostly my biology majors—become so interested in my off-campus work that they express an interest in visiting or working at the research facility.

Every adjunct faculty member is a potential link to the research, health, or allied science community, and it is a potential that is severely underdeveloped and one that can reap benefits for all the institutions and people involved. A school's adjunct faculty should be viewed as a liaison to the professional community in which its students ultimately will be seeking employment, and the college should seek to optimize those connections.

Community college students need to gain real-world experience in their fields, and they generally cannot do that on the two-year college campus. Since the adjunct faculty is a shared resource of at least two institutions and has a network of associates in both places, it is a logical conduit to facilitate the connections between the two (or more) professional facilities.

Formal arrangements between institutions may have to be made at the highest administrative levels; but the academic departments, where an understanding of the benefits such arrangements can have for their students and faculty is probably clearest, could be where the thought of outreach begins to percolate up the chain. The adjunct really is the missing link between the community college and the professional community.

Adjunct faculty members need to work together with the full-time teachers and administrators to design effective cooperative programs. It is not enough for students to visit community facilities irregularly or informally. More effective would be a program directed from the community college that allows students to register with the college and earn college credit reflecting the quality and quantity of their off-campus experience as well as some assessment of the students' performance in the program. A formal record of their participation would be useful to students who plan to transfer to four-year schools or who are seeking employment immediately after receiving their associate degrees.

An adjunct instructor's experience can also serve the full-time faculty. It is important for all faculty to be up to date in their academic fields, but the enormous volume of literature and the time constraints placed on community college teachers by heavy teaching loads makes that very difficult to do. In their midst, however, are colleagues from the worlds of research and indus-

try who can help. The adjunct could conduct professional development seminars that can be used to update and inform the department about specific research activities or other relevant information, and the pathways to local industry they help to open for the students can just as easily be traveled by faculty.

The concept of adjuncts acting as liaisons can be altered to fit the needs and interests of each college. In a well-functioning academic department, the members support one another like the links in a chain. The adjunct instructors are a vital link that can extend that educational chain to the professional community. It is time to forge that link and strengthen the chain.

**References**

Behrendt, R. L., and M. H. Parsons. 1983. "Evaluation of Part-time Faculty." In *New Directions for Community Colleges*, ed. A. Smith. San Francisco: Jossey-Bass.

Bloom, Benjamin S., ed. 1956. *Taxonomy of Educational Objectives*. New York: Longman.

Chaffee, John. 1997. *Thinking Critically*. 5th ed. New York: Houghton Mifflin.

Cruise, R. J., G. F. Furst, and R. E. Klimes. 1980. A comparison of full-time and part-time instructors at Midwestern Community College. *Community College Review* 8:52-56.

Kamps, D. 1998. The instructional quality of adjunct instructors. *Adjunct Info.* 6(Winter).

National Center for Educational Statistics. 1993. *National Study of Postsecondary Faculty*, U.S. Department of Education, Office of Educational Research and Improvement.

Statement from the conference on the growing use of part-time and adjunct faculty. 1998. *Academe* (Jan-Feb): 54-60.

Stovall, R. H. 1994. Student performance in classes taught by adjunct vs. full-time faculty. *Adjunct Info* 2(Spring).

# The Graying of Science Faculty in U.S. Colleges and Universities

## *An Unrecognized Crisis Thirty Years in the Making*

NATHAN DUBOWSKY, ELLIOTT HARTMAN, JR., LEONARD SIMONS, AND JERRY PRZYBYLSKI

Some months ago, while attending a meeting of college science educators, two of the authors (N. D. and E. H.) became acutely aware of a phenomenon that probably should have been recognized long ago. While sitting toward the back of the auditorium, we found ourselves looking over an almost solid wall of gray-haired senior faculty.

We wondered how many college science faculty are close to retirement age, and whether this "graying" of the college science faculty is a local phenomenon or if it extends nationwide. Where are the younger faculty who will continue to teach science over the next 20 or 30 years? Who will remain to mentor the younger faculty who will be appointed in the next few years? How many new faculty will be needed within the next few years to replace those soon to retire? Will there be enough younger, qualified individuals to fill the need? If there were to be a large turnover in science faculty in the next few years, how would this affect collegiate science course offerings, programs, and departmental research activities? The vast majority of current college science teachers began their careers in the 1960s at a time when student enrollments were increasing dramatically. In the late 1970s and early 1980s, college enrollments leveled off and, in some cases, declined. Some science departments even experienced budget cuts, downsizing, and faculty layoffs. Few if any new science teachers were added to the teaching faculty and few left their positions. Consequently, many current science departments are abnormally skewed toward older faculty.

> ***Column Editor's Note:*** It is appropriate, I think, in an issue that focuses on the millennium, that we pay some attention to the tendency of "time's winged chariot" to leave a bit of roadkill in its tracks.

Now, these faculty are near retirement age. At the same time total student enrollments again have begun to rise. In fact, it has been estimated that college enrollments will increase by 10 percent, or 1.5 million students, in the next decade. Moreover, the requirement that undergraduate students take one or more science courses to enhance their "science literacy" has reached just about every college campus in the nation. Therefore, it may well be necessary not only to replace retiring faculty, but also to recruit and employ additional qualified science teaching faculty to handle the anticipated increase in student population and the demand for new science courses.

There already have been some warning signs that wholesale retirements of college science teachers may be coming in the near future. A survey at Westchester Community College in 1998, designed and processed by the Higher Education Research Institute at UCLA, found that 72 percent of the teaching faculty is 50 years of age or older and that about 40 percent of this faculty considered taking early retirement in the previous two years. Predicted large-scale retirements in the elementary and secondary schools already have begun to occur.

After considering the above observations, we decided that it would be important to gather more detailed data about anticipated retirements of college science teaching faculty in the immediate future and about institutional plans for dealing with these retirements. We hypothesized that there will be an unusually higher retirement rate among college science faculty over the next five years and that colleges and universities are not prepared for the large number of retirements that we anticipate.

Two surveys to study the aging of current college science teaching faculty, what we have termed the "graying" phenomenon, were conducted in the fall of 1999. One survey (Survey A) was sent by U.S. Mail (with pre-addressed, postage-paid return envelope included) to 60 randomly selected chairs of chemistry and/or physical science departments in the New York metro-

politan area. The second survey (Survey B) was sent by e-mail to 300 randomly selected life sciences (biology) departments nationwide (100 to two-year schools and 200 to four-year colleges and universities). Both surveys were essentially the same (see **Figure 1**). They were designed to collect information about:

- the type of department and institution;
- the number of expected retirements in the upcoming year and in the next five years;
- planned replacement strategies;
- past faculty searches conducted by the department;
- difficulties anticipated in conducting faculty searches over the next five years;
- current roles of retired faculty in department activities;
- what resources the Society of College Science Teachers and other professional organizations might develop to aid in the hiring processes.

Survey A had a response rate of 43 percent while 30 percent responded to Survey B. Tables 1 and 2 summarize our findings.

The responses to Survey A (see **Table 1-Survey A**) clearly show that there will be significant numbers of faculty retirements in chemistry and physical science departments in the New York metropolitan region within the next five years. Assuming that a typical faculty member has an average professional teaching career spanning some 30 to 35 years, one would expect an average annual retirement rate of about three percent per year, provided there were a "normal" age distribution. This would translate to a 15 percent faculty retirement rate over any five-year period.

Survey A indicates that 91 percent of the community colleges in the New York metropolitan region surveyed anticipate greater than "normal" attrition due to retirements within the next five years, as do 60 percent of the four-year colleges. Only 9 percent of the community colleges report anticipating a "normal" retirement pattern. Anecdotally, one of the community colleges responded that its entire science faculty would probably retire within the next five years.

## Figure 1.

## A Study of Age Demographics of College Science Teaching Faculty in the United States.

If you are a department chair or other individual involved in the recruitment and/or employment of science teaching faculty at your college or university, we would greatly appreciate it if you would take a few minutes to complete this questionnaire, returning it to:

Dr. Nathan Dubowsky

c/o Biology Department

Westchester Community College

75 Grasslands Road, Valhalla, New York 10595

If you do not have these responsibilities, we would appreciate it if you would pass this survey on to the person who does.

The results of this survey will be included as part of a position paper submitted for publication.

Name _____

College or University _____

Address _____

_____

### School/Department Profile:

1. Department or discipline: _____

Your position _____

2. Highest degree granted by your institution:

a. Associate

b. Bachelors

c. Masters

d. Doctorate

e. other: _____

3. Institutional Affiliation:

a. Public

b. Private

4. You believe your institution is best noted for:

a. teaching excellence

b. research excellence

c. both a and b

5. Your institution provides _____ time and opportunity for faculty to do research.

a. no

b. some

c. a great deal of

6. Minimum requirement for employment in tenure track position (choose the most appropriate):

a. Master's degree with research experience

b. Master's degree with teaching experience

c. Doctorate with teaching experience

d. Doctorate with record of successful research

e. Both c and d

7. Minimum requirement for tenure (choose all that apply):

a. demonstrated teaching ability

b. demonstrated record of research and publications

c. demonstrated teaching ability and ability to direct undergraduate research

d. demonstrated teaching ability with some research and publications

e. demonstrated teaching ability but with the major emphasis on research

### Future Departmental Requirements:

1. How many faculty in your department have retired within the

a. past year _____ = _____% of total in department

b. past 5 years _____ = _____% of total in department

2. What is your best estimate of how many faculty in your department will be retiring within:

a. the next year _____ = _____ of total in department

b. the next five years _____ = _____ of total in department

3. Have there been any retirement incentives to take "early retirement" offered by your institution in the past few years?

_____ Yes

_____ No

If yes, please describe these incentives:

### Replacement Strategies:

1. For those retiring within the next five years, how do you think they will be replaced?

a. _____% Adjunct Faculty

b. _____% Full-time nontenure track primarily teaching faculty

c. _____% Full-time nontenure track primarily research faculty

d. _____% Full-time tenure track primarily teaching

e. _____% Full-time tenure track primarily research

f. _____% Will not be replaced immediately

2. What method(s) do you anticipate using to recruit new faculty?

3. How much difficulty have you had, in the past, recruiting qualified candidates for faculty positions?

a. none

b. some

c. moderate

d. considerable

e. extreme

4. What were the difficulties you encountered?

5. Please describe any difficulties you anticipate encountering in recruiting qualified individuals to fill faculty positions in your department.

6. What changes do you anticipate in your department as a result of these changes in faculty?

7. What role(s) do retired and semi-retired faculty traditionally play in your department's activities?

a. no role

b. mentoring new faculty

c. teaching courses

d. offering seminars and other special presentations

e. other: _____

8. What inducement does your department (college) offer (if any) retired faculty to continue contributing to the department and college?

### Possible Assistance From Professional Organizations:

1. What resources would you like to see developed by the Society of College Science Teachers, or other professional groups, to assist you in your faculty recruitment efforts?

2. Would you be willing to assist in the preparation of a paper resulting from this study?

a. _____ yes

b. _____ no

Another community college chemistry/physical sciences department, reporting a zero percent anticipated retirement rate in the next five years, did so because their entire science faculty had retired within the past three years and had already been replaced.

At the four-year colleges, 60 percent of respondents anticipate a similar, accelerated retirement rate, with 20 percent expecting over 50 percent retirements within the next five years. The findings of the national survey of life sciences or biology departments (see **Table 1 - Survey B**) were similar. Two-thirds of the respondents indicated that they expected between 15 percent and 40 percent of their faculty would retire in the next five years. Some predicted as many as 80 percent would retire in this time period.

When asked about how the retiring faculty would be replaced—full-time tenure track positions, full-time non-tenure track position, adjuncts, or no replacement—both surveys (see **Table 2**) showed that a clear majority of departments intended to replace most retirees with tenure-track positions. The percentage was significantly higher for four-year colleges and universities than it was for community colleges.

In fact, almost all four-year colleges and universities (92 percent) indicated that it was their intention to replace all retirees with tenure-track

## Table 1.
### Faculty Retirements Anticipated Within the Next Five Years.

Survey A. Chemistry/Physical Sciences Departments at Colleges in the New York Metropolitan Region

| % Anticipated Faculty Retirements | Community Colleges | Four-Year Colleges |
|---|---|---|
| 0-15% | 9% | 40% |
| 16-33% | 36% | 20% |
| 34-50% | 18% | 20% |
| >50% | 36% | 20% |

Survey B. Life Sciences (Biology) Departments at Colleges Nationwide

| % Anticipated Faculty Retirements | Community Colleges | Four-Year Colleges |
|---|---|---|
| 0-15% | 15% | 19% |
| 16-33% | 45% | 42% |
| 34-50% | 18% | 28% |
| >50% | 22% | 11% |

## Table 2.
### Strategies Anticipated to Replace Retiring Faculty.

| | Survey A. Chemistry and Physical Sciences Departments in New York Metropolitan Area | | Survey B. Life Science Departments Nationwide | |
|---|---|---|---|---|
| | Community Colleges | Four-Year Colleges | Community Colleges | Four-Year Colleges |
| All Full-Time Tenure Track Positions | 18% | 50% | 25% | 81% |
| Half or More Replaced by Full-Time Tenure Track Positions | 37% | 7% | 27% | 11% |
| Less Than Half Replaced by Full-Time Tenure Track Positions | 18% | 0% | 16% | 0% |
| No Replacements by Full-Time Tenure Track Positions | 27% | 43% | 32% | 8% |

positions. At the community colleges, replacement plans were markedly different. Following a nationwide trend in community colleges, there seems to be greater interest in replacing full-time faculty members with less expensive, nontenured adjuncts or "part timers."

Responses to questions about the ability to recruit qualified individuals to fill anticipated vacancies were also illuminating. Most institutions indicated that they have not had significant difficulties in recruiting science teaching faculty over the last few years and, therefore, were not anticipating significant recruiting difficulties in the immediate future.

The only possible problems that were mentioned concerned the following: attracting highly qualified individuals to institutions in "out of the way" places; competing for the most qualified applicants; finding new Ph.D.'s who had the pedagogical skills needed to make them competent classroom instructors; and, especially at research institutions, facing potential high start-up costs when hiring new research Ph.D.'s whose research interests differed significantly from those of the retiring faculty member that the new individual was to replace.

The survey did provide one possible explanation for the institutional "confidence" in recruiting new, qualified science faculty. Few institutions, especially community colleges, had any recent significant experience in faculty recruitment. Moreover, most respondents seemed unaware, or unwilling to recognize, that large numbers of retirements will occur both on their own campuses and on other college campuses, large numbers of replacements will be needed to fill the resulting vacancies, and these factors will dramatically increase competition for competent replacements.

Clearly, there will continue to be disagreements as to the actual size and qualifications of the applicant pool available to replace faculty who will soon retire. However, this admittedly small and preliminary survey clearly indicates that, within the next five years, there will be major changes in the ranks of those who will teach science in our nation's college classrooms. Many institutions will find themselves hard pressed to find sufficient numbers of qualified replacements to teach science.

In many cases, there will be shifts in departmental make-ups from a majority of tenured senior faculty to a majority of untenured junior faculty and to a higher reliance upon adjuncts and "part-timers." While most science teaching faculty replacements will have excellent academic credentials, many will lack the pedagogical skills needed to effectively transmit their knowledge to their students.

With time, these new science teachers will develop the necessary pedagogical skills. But if soon-to-retire and retired faculty members are proactive, they may be able to assist in this difficult and awkward transition process. Consequently, we recommend that:

- colleges and universities be encouraged to do long-range planning at their own institutions to define their future needs and to develop effective strategies to attract and recruit qualified science teaching personnel;

- colleges and universities be encouraged to grant official status to retired faculty so that they will be available to act as mentors and consultants to their newly hired colleagues; and,

- professional organizations, such as SCST, establish and sponsor "corps of retired college science educators" to provide advice and assistance to faculty and to science departments in transition. These kinds of services and opportunities would encourage new faculty to join science education associations and encourage retired members to continue their organizational memberships, thereby strengthening both the active members and professional societies.

### Acknowledgment

*The authors of this paper wish to thank Mrs. Ellen DiFrancesco of Westchester Community College for her help in preparing this manuscript.*

# The Counseling/Science Connection

*Integrating Mental Health Concepts and Science Content*

KATHLEEN LILLO SOWELL

 n addition to fostering academic and intellectual growth, colleges have traditionally held to missions of promoting overall student development. Their mission statements frequently reflect their commitment to (1) provide opportunities for personal development, (2) prepare students for meaningful civic participation, and (3) promote healthy lifestyles as well as cognitive goals. A holistic view of development recognizes the synergy of physical, emotional, and intellectual well-being.

Those of us who work within Student Affairs/Student Services divisions ("the other side of the house") are traditionally viewed as the ones most directly responsible for providing outside-of-class growth opportunities. The movement toward collaborative learning in the classroom, however, has awakened thoughts of new interdivisional collaborations and the development of instructional teams (Caprio, 1999). Interconnections between academic areas are becoming more common with the encouragement of writing across the curriculum, campus-wide emphasis on information literacy, and interdisciplinary centers for academic computing. Integrating counseling services with academic areas can bring yet another dimension to the developing picture of student-centered instruction.

The need for this shift exists across the entire spectrum of higher education, but is typically greater within community colleges because of the greater diversity of this population (Cohen and Brawer, 1996). I propose that to better meet the diverse academic and personal development needs of students we should move in the direction of increased cooperation between Academic Affairs and Student Services. Such collaboration has the potential to provide mutual reinforcement of student learning and growth in these areas. This paper will explain the role of campus counseling services and how it contributes to the mission of the college, examine some of the articulation points between science courses and counseling services, and offer some advantages of forging the collaborative connection.

## Role of campus counseling services

College counselors play a pivotal role in assisting students to meet personal development needs. In addition to providing direct counseling and mental health services, we frequently connect students with others on and off campus in an attempt to help solve academic-related problems. Students are seen on an appointment and walk-in basis, and counseling centers have protocols for managing the student facing a personal emergency or crisis. Counseling centers, as with other segments of the campus community, have increased accessibility to meet the schedules of the nontraditional student.

Students may seek counseling for a variety of reasons ranging from needing information regarding campus and academic policies to career counseling or assistance in dealing with a significant emotional crisis. We encourage and welcome referrals from faculty when a student is experiencing difficulty in the classroom, which may be addressed by the counseling center. Counseling personnel generally conduct outreach activities, including visiting classrooms and dormitories, in an effort to inform students of available counseling services and to provide information on specific mental health and behavioral issues.

Stated most generally, the counselor's role is to foster the academic and personal development of students. A major component of the counselor's role is to support the academic mission of the college. The efficacy of counseling centers in increasing student retention and graduation rates has empirical support (Turner and Berry, 2000; Wilson et al., 1997). Given the greater diversity of students— especially in community colleges—and budget demands (i.e., doing more with less), most educators acknowledge the benefits of collaboration between Student Services and Academic Affairs divisions. Knowing about the developmental and personal needs of college students from the counseling perspective can help classroom teachers see where they can support counselors; and knowing more about the expectations teachers have of students will empower counselors to better foster those students' academic success.

Counselors are natural collaborators. Counseling, by its very nature, is a collaborative process. The counselor and client work together to achieve attainable, mutually agreed upon goals. Every client presents a unique set of circumstances, abilities, and goals.

## Developmental needs of college students

In general, the developmental needs of college students include the mastery of tasks that challenge their current levels or capacities. These tasks may include making responsible career and lifestyle decisions, managing conflicting priorities, identifying personal values, meeting and working with individuals from diverse backgrounds, and dealing with novel situations. Community college students frequently bring additional challenges to the mastery of these tasks, including weaker academic preparation, financial stress, and stress related to the management of multiple life roles; nontraditional students, by their very nature, do not have *student* as their primary life role.

College counseling centers generally embrace a developmental rather than a clinical model of service provision. Counseling most often takes an educational approach where the counselor helps students understand how problem areas impede their academic and personal adjustment. They teach students time management skills, stress management skills, interpersonal skills, assertiveness, career decision-making, and problem-solving skills. In those centers where psychotherapy is provided (more often in four-year schools), therapy is short-term in nature. In both community colleges and four-year institutions, counselors refer students to providers off-campus when their needs exceed those that can be met by campus services. The major goal of counseling is to help empower students to make positive life changes.

## Seeking counseling assistance

Students may self-initiate contact with the center or a faculty member, or other college personnel may make a recommendation that the student seek counseling. Self-referred students may seek assistance because of poor academic performance, career and/or college major indecision, or personal situations unrelated to the academic setting but impacting their school adjustment. Many students, despite experiencing difficulty or distress, do not self-initiate contact with the counseling center. In spite of the general nonclinical approach of college counseling staff, counseling still retains a negative perception by many, and students often worry about confidentiality.

With very few exceptions, counseling is a voluntary process. Faculty and other college personnel are in a good position to identify potential student problems that may be addressed through counseling and frequently recommend to students that they visit the counseling center. We welcome and encourage such referrals and will work with faculty in any way possible to assist with this process.

Some faculty may be unsure if a student's behavior suggests a need for counseling or may be uncomfortable approaching the student with a counseling recommendation. They may be fearful of intruding or being perceived as acting in a discriminatory fashion. This is a good time for the faculty member to contact the counselor to discuss the student's behavior (anonymously if indicated), the potential benefits of counseling, and ways to approach the student. Faculty involvement can often head off greater difficulty down the road, including failure in and withdrawal from courses.

A student may more readily approach a trusted and familiar teacher or advisor regarding a personal difficulty, and that person's guidance toward appropriate services can be instrumental in the student's resolution of the problem. An expression of concern, a show of support for the student's worthiness, and information regarding resources that could be of benefit and go a long way toward encouraging the student to put forth the effort to address and resolve problems.

## What do counselors do?
Initial contacts with the student will be for the purpose of identifying the source(s) of difficulty. Does the student have inadequate study habits and/or time management skills? Are there interpersonal difficulties? Is the student overextended with family, work, personal, and/or school obligations? Are there intellectual challenges or inadequate K-12 preparation? Are there motiva-

tional or maturity issues? Are there serious mental health problems?

Students frequently come to us having inadequate decision-making and coping skills, which are causing inordinate stress. The inability to manage stress in adaptive ways leads to compromised life and health functioning and unsatisfactory academic performance, characterized by poor grades but most often by college attrition.

## Role of science teachers
Faculty frequently call upon the counseling center to assist students in resolving issues hindering academic performance. How often do we, as counselors, call upon faculty to assist us in addressing a student development or mental health need? All faculty have the potential to contribute to students' personal development. Ways to contribute include modeling healthy behavior, referring students to counselors, serving as a mentor or club advisor, and using course content to help students understand psychological health.

Social science faculty are the ones we most readily think of as teaching the courses whose content is most directly related to psychological health and interpersonal issues. Though less readily considered, science teachers, especially those who teach biological science, have an enormous amount to offer students in understanding the impact of emotional health on physical health.

Most students do not understand the relationship of mental stress and emotions to cognitive performance and physical functioning. Studies have well documented the negative impact of stress and emotional states (i.e., depression) on human physiology (Baum and Posluszny, 1999; Henderson, 1999; Spiegel, 1999). This is a novel concept to students, and it is often difficult to get them to buy into the fact that managing stress will improve their academic performance, improve and maintain their physical health, and improve their quality of life. The initial step of helping students to understand this and, thus, become motivated to do the real work of examining maladaptive strategies and adopt adaptive ones, is time-consuming. I can tell students emphatically that there are physiologic and health effects of stress and provide a very elementary explanation of how this occurs, but, as a counselor, I have neither the expertise nor the time to discuss in any depth the physiological processes that occur or that are affected by stress and negative emotions. This is an area that can be addressed more effectively in the classroom by science teachers.

Here are examples of topics appropriate to some life science curricula that also support the counselor's work:

- Immunologic and endocrinologic changes induced by stress and emotions;
- Neurophysiologic changes induced by alcohol and drugs—substances used as part of a maladaptive coping style;
- How the brain can be negatively affected by early psychological trauma and positively affected by early secure attachment; and
- How psychotherapeutic techniques such as medications and biofeedback work.

It is always difficult to add new items to course curricula, but these are topics that are taught in many introductory biology, anatomy, and physiology courses but which are sometimes given less of a real-world slant. The relevance of the biology curriculum will be underscored when students are sitting in counselors' offices and seeing the application of syllabus items to their lives.

## Benefits of collaboration

There are a number of potential benefits to integrating mental health concepts with science course content and building connections between science faculty and college counselors. At the classroom level, improved mastery and retention of science content could be expected as students have additional schemas into which to incorporate information as well as additional ways to apply the information. Individual and group counseling interventions allow opportunities for students to transfer skills and knowledge learned in the classroom. By working with counselors, faculty can gain a better understanding of students' needs, thus enhancing their teaching. By collaborating with counselors and other professionals, faculty would be modeling collaboration for their students.

At the individual level, the need to identify and address academic and quality of life impediments is reinforced by concepts learned in the classroom. Lifetime personal growth and adjustment is enhanced as students understand the interconnectedness of psychological processes and physical systems and continue the work of maintaining good health.

At the institutional level, interdivisional collaboration fosters the concept of community on campus. The mental health and personal growth of all campus personnel—not only students—is improved as the concept of mental health, as part of overall wellness, engenders greater attention across campus. Implications beyond the campus include the transmission of health empowering information to individuals who are served by alumni as they work in their chosen professions. Those professionals working in medical fields—as well as teachers and business managers or any other professionals who have responsibility for maximizing the performance of others—can be more effective in their jobs by having an understanding of the interplay of psychological and physical health factors.

Several ways in which the science teacher and college counselor can collaborate for the benefits of students include:

- Referring individual students to the counseling center;
- Counselors serving as consultants to faculty regarding managing individual students (i.e., those with discipline problems) or managing group behavior;
- Faculty serving as consultants to counselors in helping them to understand science con-

cepts including implications of new psychobiological research;

- Faculty and counselors co-leading workshops and seminars addressing health issues (i.e., stress management, anger management, substance abuse);
- Having the counselor serve as a guest speaker in the classroom where the science curriculum may be enhanced;
- Allowing/encouraging students to integrate mental health concepts into papers, and group projects utilizing the counseling center as an information resource; and
- Collaborative research between teacher and counselor.

As institutional budgets are tightened and resources become scarcer, intracampus collaborative efforts are gaining new attention. The college's mission can only be better served with greater interdivisional communication and collaboration with the outcome of students leaving school better prepared for life and career. There is an increasing awareness of the interplay of mental health and physical health, and we have an obligation as educators to ensure this information is understood by our students and that they practice healthy behaviors. College counselors and science faculty can form a natural alliance and assist students to master the concepts of health and understand the detrimental impact of maladaptive coping behaviors. At the most immediate level, good mental health can improve academic performance and college retention.

Beyond the classroom, healthy adjustment will go far to produce lifelong learners and productive citizens.

**References**

Baum, A., and D. Posluszny. 1999. Health psychology: Mapping biobehavioral contributions to health and illness. *Annual Review of Psychology* 50:137.

Caprio, M.W. 1999. Chaos and opportunity. *Journal of College Science Teaching* 28(6): 387-390.

Cohen, A.M., and F.B. Brawer. 1996. *The American Community College.* San Francisco: Jossey-Bass.

Health Reference Center. InfoTrac. Volunteer State Community College Library, Gallatin, TN. *http://infotrac.galegroup.com/itweb/tel_a_vscc.*

Henderson, C.W. 1999. Stress may increase susceptibility to infectious disease. *Immunotherapy Weekly* August 9.

Spiegel, D. 1999. Healing words: Emotional expression and disease outcome. *The Journal of the American Medical Association* April 14, p. 1328.

Turner, A.L., and T.R. Berry. 2000. Counseling center contributions to student retention and graduation: A longitudinal assessment. *Journal of College Student Development* 41(6): 627-636.

Wilson, S.B., T.W. Mason, and J.J.M. Ewing. 1997. Evaluating the impact of receiving university-based counseling services on student retention. *Journal of Counseling Psychology* 44:316-320.

# Navigating the Standards

## A Preview of the College-Level "Pathways to the Science Standards"

M. W. CAPRIO

The *National Science Education Standards* (NRC, 1996) have been the most discussed topic among science educators since the National Research Council began working on the project in 1994.

The Standards address the K-12 level, but the *Journal of College Science Teaching (JCST)*—which targets readers with a special interest in college-level courses—has frequently examined issues from the *Standards*. Why? Why is a K-12 document of such interest to the college community? There are several answers to this question.

The importance of the Standards for colleges rests on the fact that the NRC work will ultimately result in a profound restructuring of K-12 science education. The outcome is that our traditional college courses will no longer be an appropriate match for entering students. These students, who will have received a standards-based science education in their precollege years, will be prepared to construct knowledge through inquiry and will be primed for something more than passive participation in lectures and "cook-book" laboratories.

A second reason college science teachers need to be concerned about the Standards is because the key to successful implementation of these guidelines rests with tomorrow's K-12 teachers who are students in *our* classes today. We must consider, too, that these teachers will teach much as they themselves were taught (Goodlad, 1990; Sheingold and Hadley, 1990). We can help ensure that tomorrow's teachers will be likely to teach according to the new science standards (NRC, 1996, 27-53) by making a special effort to break the old mold and teach students today as they will be expected to teach tomorrow.

As compelling as these motives may be for college instructors to connect their teaching practices to the K-12 science standards, there is a third issue that, I think, carries more weight than either of the first two.

The first two points (i.e., aligning collegiate science education with our students' K-12 preparation and needing to be mindful of our preservice teachers) are of a practical nature, but our third reason for attending to the Standards is more philosophical. It speaks of the Standards as a shared value system for all science educators.

The Standards were the outcome of a national dialog on science education. Never before has there been such a well organized and extensive discussion of what our nation wants and needs for the science education of its young people. The exchange involved some of America's leading scientists, business leaders, educational administrators, and teachers on all levels. Nearly 150 people participated directly and many times that number contributed through their professional societies. After the draft of the Standards was prepared, it was mailed to thousands of interested individuals for their input before the NRC made the final revision.

The Standards are a statement of what we, as a nation, value in science education. It is the closest declaration we have ever had to a national ethic for science education. These are our common values on science literacy distilled from our long, national debate. As such, the Standards empower us because when people share a vision derived from common values they are usually capable of more productive action.

College teachers were well represented in the dialog, and played a major role in shaping the ethic that emerged from it. K-12 may be the explicit focus of the Standards, but all science education is connected and so the guidelines affect the entire spectrum.

It is true, however, that the language and examples in the Standards are often pointed toward a K-12 audience. Sometimes that wrongly suggests that they may not be germane to higher education. In addition, there are cultural and institutional differences between the various educational strata, and those differences also help obscure the implications the Standards have for college teachers.

To facilitate the translation of the Standards into a college context and make it more useful for college teachers, the College Committee of the National Science Teachers Association (NSTA) is creating a document to help college science teachers and administrators navigate the Standards more easily. The book includes chapters and essays contributed by many people. Eleanor Siebert, the former director of NSTA's College Division, and Bill McIntosh, the current director, are the editors. The title is *College Pathways to the Science Education Standards*.

We have the permission of the editors to print the *Pathways* table of contents and preface here to give *JCST* readers a preview of what will come. At the time I wrote this *JCST* article (mid-October), the *Pathways* manuscript was at a point in its development where any major changes were unlikely, but it was still in draft form.

### References

NRC (National Research Council). 1996. *National Science Education Standards* Washington, D.C.: National Academy Press.

Goodlad, J. I. 1990. *Teachers for Our Nation's Schools*. San Francisco, CA: Jossey-Bass.

Sheingold, K., and M. Hadley. 1990. *Accomplished Teachers: Integrating Computers into Classroom Practice*. New York: Bank Street College of Education, Center for Technology in Education.

## College Pathways to the Science Education Standards
## Table of Contents

**PREFACE**

**INTRODUCTION**
A Vision of Science Literacy:
Science Education for All

**CHAPTER 1**
Teaching Standards
*William J. McIntosh, Coordinator*

**Introduction**
**Standard A:** Planning an Inquiry-Based Science Program
• *Changing Student Attitudes About Science Through Inquiry-Based Learning*
**Standard B:** Guiding and Facilitating Learning
**Standard C:** Linking Assessing, Learning, and Teaching
• *Assessment Techniques to Guide Teaching in Courses with Large Enrollments*
**Standard D:** Designing and Managing the Learning Environment
• *Developing Experimental Design Skills of Students*
**Standard E:** Building Learning Communities
• *Creating a Learning Community in Introductory Biology*
**Standard F:** Participating in Program Development
• *Aligning Courses for Standards-Based Teaching*

**CHAPTER 2**
Professional Development Standards
*Joseph I. Stepans, Coordinator*

**Introduction**
**Standard A:** Learning Science Content
• *Caltech Precollege Science Initiative (CAPSI)*
**Standard B:** Learning to Teach Science
• *Vignette from a Center for Teaching Excellence: Developing Courses for Elementary Education Majors*
• *University of Wyoming Elementary Education Curriculum Reform*

**Standard C:** Learning to Learn
• *The LEAD Center at the University of Wisconsin-Madison*
**Standard D:** Designing Professional Development Programs
• *Preparing Future Faculty*
• *Designing Professional Development Experiences for K-12 Teachers*
• *The WyTRIAD Professional Development Process*

**CHAPTER 3**
Assessment Standards
*Judith E. Heady, Coordinator*

**Introduction**
**Standard A:** Coordination with Intended Purposes
• *Structured Study Groups: Using Peer-Facilitated Instruction to Develop Self-Assessment Skills*
• *Literature-Based Examinations and Grading Them: Well Worth the Effort*
• *The Counter-Intuitive Event: A Performance-Based Assessment*
**Standard B:** Measuring Student Achievement and Opportunity to Learn
• *Using Journals to Assess Student Understanding of Anatomy and Physiology*
• *Teaching Without Exams Through the Use of Student-Generated Portfolios in an Undergraduate Environmental Geology Class*
**Standard C:** Matching Technical Quality of Data with Consequences
• *Effective Use of Pretests and Post-tests*
• *Using Assessment in Curriculum Reform*
**Standard D:** Avoiding Bias
• *Using Student Strengths to Develop Assessment Tools for Nonscience Majors*
**Standard E:** Making Sound Inferences
• *Portfolio Assessment*
• *Assessment Criteria as a Heuristic for Developing Student Competency in Analysis and Evaluation of Published Papers in the Sciences*

## College Pathways to the Science Education Standards Preface

*WANTED: College and university science teachers wishing to become engaged in a comprehensive, important, and potentially transforming educational movement. Those who accept the challenge will join with precollege teachers in a quest to gift every American with essential understanding of the physical and biological processes that characterize our world, and to nurture curiosity and scientific habits of mind. In the process, all participants will experience change and renewal.*

\* \* \*

A job announcement such as that above might describe what is in store for higher education faculty who internalize the principles and practices recommended by the *National Science Education Standards* (*NSES*). The job is so important, in fact, that the *NSES* has special significance for higher education science faculty.

Significant reform attention is focused on science education because so many Americans—from children to adults—do not have a correct understanding of basic science concepts and are, therefore, ill-equipped to make critical decisions, such as those related to health and medicine, the environment, and biotechnology. More sadly, they are unable to appreciate the intricate wonder that is our Earth.

Another driving force of the reform movement is the accelerating need for individual and national competence and competitiveness in a global economy that is increasingly based on science and technology. As postsecondary teachers of science, we cannot be complacent in the belief that what we have always done will enable our future adults to compete in this world. Mediocre science scores on international achievement tests such as the *Third International Mathematics and Science Study* (*TIMSS*) underscore the need for a comprehensive approach to changing the way that science is taught and learned.

The *National Science Education Standards* provide a comprehensive guide as we move toward achieving a scientifically literate nation. These standards are based on our current, research-based understanding of the teaching-and-learning process, common perceptions (including misperceptions) of scientific concepts, and the role of prior knowledge in learning. Hundreds of teachers, scientists, science educators, and administrators from across the country collaborated on the *NSES*, which suggest both what students should know and be able to do at each developmental level and how we can align curriculum, instruction, and assessment to help them achieve these expectations. The *NSES* also address systemic issues of teacher preparation, professional development, the quality of school programs, and the entire educational system as a context for K-12 reform.

University and college professors of science are an integral part of this educational system because it is, in very large part, from our courses that society will learn its science. The lessons and experiences we provide will be passed to future generations—by way of our majors who enter fields of science and technology, as well as by way of those nonmajors who make policy and those who approve it. The *NSES* ask that we approach this task differently than we have in the past. Among the most important students in our university classrooms are those preparing to become K-12 teachers. The responsibility of preparing teachers lies primarily with higher education, and here science faculty and those in education each have important roles. The responsibility of science faculty members is not only to develop the science knowledge of our students, but also their understanding of the nature of science, their ability to understand and use scientific ways of thinking, and their ability to make connections and apply what they know to the world outside the science classroom. The responsibility of education faculty members is not only to provide fundamental information and skills related to teaching and learning, but also to mentor teachers in their ability to actively study and reflect on what they do and use their own research to make informed decisions about the appropriateness of curriculum instruction and assessment in their own classrooms.

The purpose of this *Pathways* guide is to present and interpret the *NSES* in ways that are meaningful to higher education faculty members, especially those who teach science. The teaching and assessment standards (Chapters 1 and 3) are the focal points of the book. The professional development standards (Chapter 2) as presented in this book carry a dual message. First the standards speak to science faculty about ways to develop teaching skills so as to maximize learning opportunities for our students; second, the standards serve as a guide to faculty members who are involved in providing professional development, emphasizing deep learning and genuine conceptual change rather than superficial exposures. The content standards (Chapter 4) are foundations upon which college instruction can build. Each chapter is organized around a set of common standards. A short essay addresses the implications for college science teaching. For those interested in pursuing further the concepts developed in this book, references to supporting articles are included.

We have tried to maintain the original emphasis of the *NSES* and to convey their central vision. We agree that at the college level as well as K-12 *all* students can learn science; consequently, suggestions for teaching nonscience majors and students with special needs are included. We also believe that science should be an active process that engages students both intellectually and physically—*especially* at the introductory level. To illustrate this approach, we have asked colleagues to share ways they have structured courses for maximum student involvement.

*College Pathways to the Science Education Standards* is full of ideas, examples, and suggestions. As such, it is an appropriate resource for many audiences. It will be useful to high school teachers of advanced placement courses as well as postsecondary faculty. There is no one way to use this resource. Our hope is that it will raise questions and stimulate thinking about what and how we teach, and how we might study and improve what we do. We hope it will elevate consideration of the implications of the *NSES* for postsecondary science teaching and, in so doing, encourage each reader to develop and grow in understanding of the teaching-and-learning process.

# Designing Nonmajors' Science Courses—Is There a Better Way?

*A Different Approach to Developing Science Courses for Nonscience Majors*

M. W. CAPRIO

Scientific literacy is a reasonable enough name for our goal but, in some ways, referring to the bulk of our course content as *scientific* overemphasizes its academic specialization and is misleading to students.

Science literacy courses (typically those courses earmarked in college catalogs as being for nonscience majors) rarely present any content on the cutting edge of the discipline. All we ever expect students to learn about science is a bit about the process itself and a few principles and concepts that have long since moved from the pure scientists' domain to the pages of the popular press and into the realm of what we can more properly call the *body of cultural knowledge.*

When students read Darwin's *The Origin of Species*, for example, they are learning very basic biology through a piece of nineteenth-century literature that could arguably have a place in the English curriculum. And although Mendelian genetics may be exemplary biology, it is biology that is well over a century old. This is the kind of science that educated nonscientists know as much for its historical significance as for its scientific value.

Science is something that we humans do, and we ultimately integrate the information we derive from our scientific endeavors with the whole of our knowledge to help us make sense of our complex world.

> *Program Standard B from the* National Science Education Standards: *The program of study in science for all students should be developmentally appropriate, interesting, and relevant to students' lives; emphasize student understanding through inquiry; and be connected with other school subjects.*
>
> —(NRC, 1996, 212)

Darwin, Shakespeare, Mendel, Melville, Newton, Aristotle, Einstein, Michaelangelo: their work and that of so many others is fundamental to our cultural heritage. When we emphasize the *scientific* nature of such basic subject matter we suggest it has some specialized value of little relevance to the nonmajor's world.

Am I suggesting that the work of Darwin, Mendel, Newton, and other authors of our course content has somehow moved across campus and into the humanities division, and that we should change what we call the subject matter in introductory science courses and give it a name other than *science*? Of course not. What I do think we need to do, however, is to be intellectually honest with our students and ourselves: what we are exposing students to in our science literacy courses is that part of the cultural fabric that originally came from scientific pursuits but that is now fundamental to the world view of scientists and nonscientists alike. We need to recognize, and our students need to understand, that most of the topics we teach to nonmajors represent what is actually the scientific literacy component of a broader and more general *cultural literacy*.

Program Standard B says that science programs "should be . . . interesting and relevant to students' lives . . . and be connected with other school subjects." When we begin to think of science topics as more than just *scientific* literacy, when we can appreciate science as an essential component in the cultural framework of our lives, we begin to see the far-reaching implications of this standard.

In his book, *Science and Human Values*, Jacob Bronowski talks about a person needing both a scientific and humanistic perspective of the world in order to approach an accurate sense of reality. Bronowski's book powerfully and beautifully supports the liberal arts tradition. Educated people know the value of this composite point of view and yet educators routinely compartmentalize the disciplines, assuming that some magical synthetic process will occur in our students to create the desired holistic view of knowl-

edge, hopefully before they graduate. (We are not stopping here to examine to what degree the synthesis that we hope for our students has actually occurred in ourselves.) Even in our nonmajors' courses, we usually cling to our specializations and rarely help students to integrate the scientific and the humanistic. To a degree, constructivism in education appears to let us dodge this issue.

We often describe constructivism in education as an approach that allows students to integrate new information—in this case scientific information—into their existing cognitive frameworks. The business major would have a different cognitive framework than someone majoring in music; and, to complicate matters, no two business or music majors would be expected to be identical in this respect. It seems, on the surface, that in constructivism we can stick to our specializations and still claim to have a wonderfully individualistic approach to education, with the students bearing most of the responsibility for the individualization. But, no, not really.

Constructing knowledge is not a process we can *allow* students to do on their own. It is true that we expect students to take more responsibility for their own learning with a constructivist approach, but this is not to say that we entirely abrogate our responsibility for all but dispensing the subject matter of science. In fact, when we promise our students the fruits of constructivism we are assuming significantly *more* responsibility than when we practice as traditionalists and only have to guarantee short-term retention and superficial understanding.

And, too, with constructivism, the teacher's task has also become much more technically complex. Every student comes to us with a different cognitive framework into which they seek to integrate what we have for them, and—according to what we know about the abysmal level of science literacy in this country—we have to assume they have very little experience or ability accomplishing that with scientific subject matter.

If constructivism is to fulfill its promise, the "guide on the side" needs to be very knowledgeable about those cognitive constructs sitting at the desks in his or her classroom. It may not be possible, or even desirable, to get inside the students' heads on the level of their personal intellects; but, if our constructivist dreams are to become reality, the science teacher should, at the very least, know enough about the nonscience academic areas to be useful in assisting students as they strive to make the connections we expect of them.

A broad interpretation of Program Standard B urges us to define the "science program" for nonmajors (and maybe for science majors, too) in larger, cultural terms. Depending on their academic majors, most nonscience majors take one, two, or occasionally three natural science courses. With so little science in their academic lives, it is easy for these students to endure the hardship, the way an agnostic might endure a compulsory church service, and remain unchanged by the experience. Only if we can integrate their science experience with the mainstream of our students' lives and give it meaning and purpose for them will there be any possibility that they will retain and enlarge the lessons they recite so well on our exams.

The reality, though, is that we are not all Jacob Bronowskis, and as much as we would like to think of ourselves as broad-based scholars, we are clearly more comfortable in our own disciplines and are usually wise enough to remain quietly unassuming about nonscientific things. But when we begin to think of the topics of nonmajors' science as having been woven over time into the cultural fabric of our society, we have to realize that if we teach these topics purely as science—without their cultural connectives— we are belying their full significance, and we probably ought to consider altering our stance a bit. But how?

Maybe we, as scientists, are too close to science to be left alone to teach it to nonmajors. That sounds contradictory and reminds me of von Clausewitz's dictum that "war is too important to be left to the generals"; but could it be true that science education for nonscience majors is too important—and maybe even a little too complicated now, with its cultural accoutrements and constructivist goals—to be left entirely to the scientists? How can we at once admit that we are unfamiliar with the cognitive structures of the disciplines into which our science must integrate in the minds of our students and, at the same time, claim to be the guide that will help those students effect that integration?

I think we need an approach to curriculum development for nonmajors' science courses that will achieve a better fit between the scientific subject matter and the cognitive frameworks of nonscientist students, and I think I have an idea about how we can do it. My solution seems too simple to be right, it is based on a tried-and-true classroom technique, it acts on some advice from the professor of my senior capstone course called *Techniques of Biological Research*, and it automatically incorporates a professional development program that could help ensure the successful implementation of the curriculum it produces.

The classroom technique it emulates is collaborative, minds-on learning; the advice from the professor that it follows is that the quickest way to get an answer to a question you have is to "ask someone who knows"; and the professional development component is just an outgrowth of the institution's extant collegiality, and its value will be proportional to the vitality and magnitude of that commodity.

The impression of science out there vacillates between it being done by a white-coated elite or by gnome-like creatures with pocket protectors who sometimes use duct tape to repair their eyeglasses. And the general public generally believes that it cannot understand science and is not sure that it even wants to understand it. Of course that is simply not true: scientific thinking and scientific information is used fairly regularly by many nonscientists without them even being aware of it (Gould, 1997).

One discussion of scientific literacy held at the *1997 Lilly Conference Northwest* recognized how scientific thinking permeates other disciplines. The Lilly Conference Northwest was part of a project conducted by the Women's Studies Program and the Center for Science Education at Portland State University (PSU) and funded by the Association of American Colleges and Universities, entitled *Women and Scientific Literacy: Building Two-Way Streets*. Here is a brief summary of that discussion (Lilly Conference, 1997).

Consider the following "habits of mind" often mentioned as essential to scientific literacy (an example of a discipline outside the natural sciences that we consider to share the particular habit of mind are in parentheses): (1) skepticism, a tolerance for ambiguity and openness to new and revised claims (all scholarly disciplines); (2) understand how to test claims against evidence (all scholarly disciplines); (3) be able to understand causation/correlation and the difference between them (sociology); (4) understand certain concepts such as rates of change and proportion (epidemeology); (5) be able to use and understand mathematics as a language for expressing relationships and patterns (logic).

Most of us can probably expand and strengthen the point of this summary by adding disciplines and subdisciplines to the parenthetical lists that accompany items three, four, and five, above. One goal of the PSU project is to "... convince nonscience faculty that scientific ideas can easily be integrated into their general studies courses" (Lilly Conference, 1997). What I am about to suggest is related to this concept but is a little different from it.

## What if . . .
Instead of making an effort to show the uniqueness of the scientific way of knowing, what if we were to work at emphasizing the similarities between science and the nonscience disciplines? What if we were to establish curriculum development committees for our nonscience courses that included nonscience faculty?

The point would not be to design interdisciplinary courses but to construct in the scientists and nonscientists an understanding of where the articulation points are in their cognitive frameworks. We would not have to start from ground zero here: a rich literature reporting the differences and similarities of the various disciplinary cultures already exists (for example: Elmers, 1999; Donald, 1995; Gaff and Wilson, 1971; Becher, 1989; Biglan, 1973). This collaboration is the professional development part of the package. Will this help us, as scientists, better understand the nonscientific habits of mind; and will we, as colleagues, come to appreciate the likenesses we all share?

Would this committee actually design a science course? I don't know. It might just wrestle with the issues that separate (unite?) the two cultures. Then the scientists might go off with their new knowledge to develop a course for their nonmajors that would be different than anything they would have been able to develop before having such a collaborative experience. And could these discussions have a similar effect on the non-scientists?

When I think of the goal of the PSU program, when I consider the scientific thinking that I know nonscientists engage in all the time, and when I contemplate the pleasure of engaging my humanist colleagues in discussions about science education, I find that I am beginning to see Program Standard B as an opportunity for growth.

## Other ideas?
What I have brainstormed here represents a different way of approaching the development of science courses for nonscience students. It recognizes that we share our nonscience majors with other academic divisions, and it utilizes col-

laboration with nonscience faculty to identify articulation points between the science and the nonscience disciplines in order to equip the science teachers better to guide their nonscience students in the construction and assimilation of new scientific knowledge. But there may be other ways of achieving the same ends.

I invite readers with thoughts to share on approaches to the development of curriculum for nonscience majors to write to me. We will happily devote space in a future column to their short comments or full articles. I am looking forward to the contributions.

## References

Becher, T. 1989. *Academic Tribes and Territories: Intellectual Enquiry and the Cultures of Disciplines*. Philadelphia: Open University Press.

Biglan, A. 1973. Relationship between subject matter, characteristics and the structure and output of university departments. *Journal of Applied Psychology* 57:204-13.

Donald, J. 1995. Disciplinary differences in knowledge validation. In *Disciplinary Differences in Teaching and Learning: Implications for Practice*, eds. N. Hativa and M. Marincovich. San Francisco: Jossey-Bass.

Elmers, M. 1999. Working with faculty from different disciplines. *About Campus* March/April.

Gaff, J., and R. Wilson. 1971. Faculty cultures and interdisciplinary cultures. *Journal of Higher Education* 42:186-201.

Gould, S. 1997. Drink deep, or taste not the pierian spring. *Natural History* 106:24-26.

Lilly Conference Northwest. 1997. Internet: http://horizons.sb2.pdx.edu/~fem-sci-lit/lilly.html.

National Research Council. 1996. *National Science Education Standards*. Washington, D.C.: National Academy Press.

# Designing Science Literacy Courses

## *A Recipe for a Successful Science Course That's Sure to Please*

ART HOBSON

n response to M. W. Caprio's invitation (Caprio, 1999), I would like to share some thoughts about designing science literacy courses. We must bring such courses to *all* of our students. Every college campus and every high school should offer a variety of science courses aimed primarily at the nonscientists who form the great bulk of our student populations.

The reason is simple: they vote. An industrialized democracy cannot survive in this scientific age unless the bulk of its population is scientifically literate. The wreckage caused by a scientifically illiterate citizenry is all around us in the form of uninformed choices about energy, the environment, education, pseudoscientific pursuits, and much else.

There are many other reasons, involving competitiveness, jobs, culture, and the health of our own scientific professions. For example, the dreadful U.S. physics and math showing on the twelfth grade Third International Mathematics and Science Study (TIMSS) is not surprising given that the great majority of high school students has never had and never will have a single physics course (Neuschatz and McFarling, 1999).

I recommend two key methodological ingredients and two key content-oriented ingredients for a successful liberal-arts science course. First,

make it nontechnical, that is, conceptual. Nonscientists have no need and even less desire to learn the technical jargon and mathematical techniques needed for original scientific work. Focus on the broad concepts, and eliminate unnecessary jargon and techniques. I hasten to add, however, that nonscientists do need *numeracy*. They should become comfortable with powers of 10, the metric system, graphs, probabilities, percentages, numerical estimates, error bounds, and quantitative measurements.

Second, teach in an interactive, inquiry-oriented way. For example, peer instruction (Mazur, 1997; Meltzer and Manivannan, 1996) works wonderfully even in my large (up to 250) lecture classes. This method is based on multiple-choice "concept test" questions carefully designed to stimulate thought, correct misconceptions, extend knowledge, and promote discussion.

The instructor puts a question on the projection screen, and students discuss it with their neighbors (perhaps with some coaching) and then indicate their individual answers by some immediate feedback mechanism such as large hand-held cards labeled "A, B, . . . ". If the answers suggest a lack of understanding, the instructor might discuss the topic further and ask the question again. Interactive teaching can be used during some, much, or all of any given lecture. Among its many benefits, it encourages students to verbalize their reasoning. It's heartening to see an entire class of nonscientists talking about science!

Third, include plenty of the modern science that defines today's scientific world view. Science literacy courses should be nontechnical, but precisely for that reason they can be *more* conceptually sophisticated and contemporary than the technical courses for science majors. For instance in my own field, physics, nonscientists are fascinated by, and quite capable of grasping, the special and general theories of relativity, "nonlocality" and other quantum subtleties, quantum field theory, the accelerating expansion of the universe, dark matter, and much more. For confirmation, simply ask yourself which science books the non-scientific public reads. A recent example (Greene, 1999) presents basic concepts of general relativity and quantum physics and their blending to form "string theory," a theory of all four fundamental forces. Without oversimplification, and without mathematical or other technicalities, Greene presents these new developments in a manner that nonscientists can grasp if they are willing to read attentively.

Finally, make it socially relevant. Connect science with the current world by including such issues as bioethics, pollution, energy efficiency, climate change, nuclear power, overpopulation, food resources, water resources, technological risk, pseudoscience, weapons of mass destruction, communication, and computerization. Such topics fascinate students, they bring home the relevance of science to students' own lives, they make excellent vehicles for science teaching, and they are surely important in their own right.

These four ingredients have been successful in our physics literacy course, regardless of who has taught that course. In large numbers, and despite the scary *physics* title, students choose this course over competing science courses. Student evaluations are remarkably high despite frequent comments that the course is difficult.

And there is some evidence that the lectures are effective in transmitting physics knowledge. If the lectures are effective, then one would expect students who attend regularly to learn more than students who do not attend regularly. Using attendance records and scores from the comprehensive final exam, I was able to check this prediction.

In the fall of 1998, attendance was checked on 22 occasions. Defining "high attenders" as students who missed not more than three times out of the 22, and defining "low attenders" as students who missed at least half the time, the distribution of scores was about 15 percentage points higher for high attenders than for low attenders. The average scores of the high and low attenders were 71 percent and 55 percent respectively, a difference of about 1.5 letter grades. In the spring of 1999, the same two attendance groups averaged 66 percent and 56 percent on the final exam, a difference of one letter grade. Although some of this difference might stem from differences in the natural abilities of the two groups, it seems likely that at least some of the difference stems from class attendance. Readers can contact me for copies of the detailed data.

## References

Caprio, M. W. 1999. Designing nonmajors' science courses—Is there a better way? *Journal of College Science Teaching* 29:134-137.

Greene, Briane. 1999. *The Elegant Universe.* New York: W. W. Norton and Company.

Mazur, Eric. 1997. *Peer Instruction.* Upper Saddle River, NJ: Prentice Hall.

Meltzer, D. E., and K. Manivannan. 1996. Promoting interactivity in physics lecture classes. *The Physics Teacher* 34:72-76.

Neuschatz, M., and M. McFarling. 1999. *High School Physics for a New Millennium.* American Institute of Physics Report, July, p. 42.

# Teaching to Learn

*Why Should Teachers Have*
*All the Fun?*

MARIO W. CAPRIO AND DEBRA S. BORGESEN

t is a rare teacher who has not arrived at new and deeper insights about the discipline while teaching it. The education literature, as well as conventional wisdom dating back at least to the time of Seneca in the first century A.D., recognizes teaching to be a powerful learning modality (Renkl, 1997; Skinner, 1994; Berliner, 1989; Whitman, 1988). Peer-tutoring programs and classroom activities where students do limited teaching of assigned course topics apply this teaching-to-learn principle to motivate and enhance instruction.

Service learning—where students put into practice their course work in a real-world setting and combine experiential learning with community service (Wiegand and Strait, 2000)—is a well-grounded approach to teaching and learning. Frequently touted as a child of the 1990s, service learning bears close kinship to "learning by experience," which has its roots much earlier in the century (Dewey, 1997) and that, in fact, may be the most ancient learning model of all.

In this paper, we describe teaching-to-learn activities in a community service setting involving three very different groups of students: (1) nonscience majors in an evening section of an introductory natural science course (SCI 100) at

Volunteer State Community College (VSCC); (2) middle school students at the Murrell School; and (3) a Cub Scout pack of home-schooled, elementary-school-aged children. VSCC is a comprehensive community college of about 7,000 students in Gallatin, Tennessee, a suburb of Nashville; the Murrell School is a Nashville inner-city middle school serving students with severe behavioral problems; and the home-schooled Cub Scouts (who participated with parents and siblings of both sexes) were from a rural Tennessee community and included children from eight to twelve years old.

## Why we did it

Organizing science course content in a coherent way is an essential step toward comprehension. Coherent organization makes it easier to study a subject and easier to apply it to new situations. Without logical organization students see science courses as little more than random collections of facts that defy understanding and that can only be mastered through memorization. But designing presentations for conceptual understanding and delivering those lessons carefully does not necessarily mean that students will retain what seems so clear to them in the lecture hall (Bonwell and Eison, 1991; McKeachie et al., 1986).

Teachers get a great deal of practice organizing the course content, making sense of it, developing alternative explanations of it, and inventing analogies and mnemonic devices to facilitate its understanding and retention. This is also the way we would like students to process the subject matter, but they usually do not. We suspected that if we shifted some of the intellectual activities of teaching to the students, they might model our behavior and share in some of the learning dividends that we receive (Whitman, 1988).

A second reason for trying a teaching-to-learn approach was that we have learned from the students themselves that while science may not be terribly interesting to them, they are interested in education. They know that if they are not parents already, they probably will be, and that parents are teachers. Therefore, knowing more about teaching might make them better at parenting. They also want to learn more about teaching because they are participants in formal education, and they can get more out of the experience by better understanding the process.

Science education learning and study skills (e.g., scientific literacy, problem-solving approaches, study methods, presentation of subject matter, and exam preparation) support lifelong learning as well as students' immediate needs in the classroom.

## What we did in the SCI 100 class

As part of the course introduction on the first day of class, we informed the SCI 100 students that their course would include several teaching-to-learn projects. Students began by completing specific readings in the *National Science Education Standards* (NRC, 1996) then, in collaborative groups, designed an inquiry-based lesson about a particular property of matter. We gave them a list of the necessary details involved in the assignment to guide their work.

The collaborative groups presented their lessons to the class, suggested assessment strategies,

and peer tutored their topic to students requiring assistance. The instructor facilitated their presentations, from assisting with multi-media aids to supplementing or clarifying the subject matter where appropriate. After each presentation, we reviewed the subject matter and explored its implications, discussed the strengths and weakness of the lesson, and talked about how to modify it for a younger audience.

## At the Murrell School

Before the semester began, we spoke with administrators at the Murrell School and at VSCC to obtain permission for the college students to visit the middle school to present science lessons. With the peer presentations over, we explained the Murrell School project to the SCI 100 students. This off-campus adventure was handled as an extra credit opportunity for those who would be able to participate. (Community college students often have restrictive work and/or family schedules that make it difficult to require attendance at events outside of regularly scheduled classes.)

Students at Murrell follow the regular education core curriculum for the Davidson County School District. To prepare for the teaching-to-learn project, the Murrell teacher discussed with students the properties of matter, laboratory safety, and scientific instruments, as outlined in the curriculum. This enabled students to better understand the subject matter the college students would be presenting and taught them how to treat equipment, which was new to them, safely.

Preparation also included teaching social skills. Since the Murrell students have encountered numerous social as well as academic failures throughout their education, it is imperative that they learn social skills as part of their daily instruction, such as introducing oneself, using social courtesies, and welcoming a visitor to their classroom.

Upon arriving at the Murrell School, the cooperating teacher met the college students at a time when the middle school students were still in their physical education class, allowing the college students to set up the work stations. They arranged four work stations, each dealing with a different property of matter and each having a hands-on activity. When the students returned from the gym, their teacher introduced the college students and explained the activities. As they moved from station to station, the middle school students talked with the college students about the subject matter and the activities. The students were engaged in the science activities for more than one hour. Their teacher distributed certificates of completion to the children that the college students had left.

Owing to the special needs and the behavioral problems of the students at the Murrell School, the class has only seven students. An assistant and a social worker are also present in the room with the teacher. Having assistants in the classroom allowed the teacher to take time to talk with the college students after the lesson about special education as a career.

## With home schoolers

A third opportunity for teaching-to-learn occurred when we brought a group of home-schooled children to the college for a "Science Expo." In this case the SCI 100 students planned and executed the entire event. The collaborative

groups set up six inquiry stations in the lab while two students from the class escorted the children and their parents on a tour of the campus. Each station offered a different hands-on lesson consisting of several activities that was part of the SCI 100 curriculum but tailored to the eight-to twelve-year-old visitors.

Upon returning from their tour, the children moved at their own rate through each inquiry station and received a check mark on their program cards after they successfully completed the lesson. When they finished the circuit, the SCI 100 students awarded certificates of completion and a gift packet (assembled by the college public relations office) to the participants.

With minor variations, we followed this program for SCI 100 students for two consecutive semesters last year.

## Impact on those involved

We initially called this subtitle "Impact on students," but that turned out to be much too narrow. These teaching-to-learn activities have affected the classroom teachers, administrators, community college, parents of the students, as well as the students themselves.

For both the Murrell School activity and the Science Expo, the college students had a clear sense of service. They felt they were using their new scientific knowledge to do something good for someone. When the guests had left and they were cleaning up after the Science Expo, one student remarked, "I really think we made a difference in these kids' lives." That comment seemed to express the feelings of the group. These nonscience majors—perhaps for the first time—took pride in having and using scientific knowledge.

The college students mastered a topic that was difficult for them and applied their new knowledge to a real-world situation. This validated their competence and reinforced their self-confidence with scientific subject matter. Self-confidence and a sense of personal competence are important motivators of learning (Caprio, 1993a and 1993b; Wlodkowski, 1985).

In the spring 2000 semester, three students changed their majors to education after the Science Expo. Two of these became elementary education majors and the third decided he wanted to be a high school science teacher. After the Murrell experience, the participating students and their instructor met for lunch on the way back to the VSCC campus. There was the sense of a bond forming among the students and the instructor that did not develop with other members of the class.

On the next major SCI 100 exam after the Murrell visit and before the Science Expo, the students who participated in the Murrell project did significantly better than the class average, although that was not true of the class in general. This observation was consistent both semesters.

The benefits of the teaching-to-learn program extended beyond classroom walls. The Murrell students also engaged in teaching-to-learn: they applied their new knowledge and feelings of success to teaching classmates who had been absent on the day of the visit.

Later, Murrell School administrators invited Professor Caprio to be a judge at the school-wide science fair. During his evaluation of the science fair projects, he provided positive feedback to each student, which increased their feelings of

success in a school setting and their comfort with science topics. The Murrell students in the class the college students visited displayed enthusiasm for the school's science fair, and the quality of their projects benefited from their exposure to the college students. Some of the students chose to model their "college teachers" by performing experiments similar to the ones the college students had demonstrated.

After learning about the college students' visit, other classroom teachers at the Murrell School requested copies of the science activities that the visitors brought. Murrell students do not often have an opportunity to speak with college students, and this visit provided them with an uncommon social experience as well as information about their local community college.

The Murrell students have been removed from mainstream schools because of their disruptive behavior, and they have experienced frequent failures in school and at home. Poor self-esteem and extremely low self-confidence are the inevitable consequences of chronic failure. That college students took the time to come to the school and work with them told the Murrell students that they were valued. This activity promoted feelings of success and self-worth that are very beneficial to emotionally disturbed children. The children's exemplary social behavior during this experience was clear evidence that the structure of this academic exercise was also meeting emotional needs.

The on-campus Science Expo during the spring semester differed from the fall event in that it included participation of division and department administrators and a counselor from the student services department of the college. As a result of that session, administrative support is now available for a larger version of the Science Expo and will involve college students from the majors' as well as nonmajors' courses. The event will also be opened to elementary students from the wider community. At this writing, plans are underway to institutionalize what began as a classroom teaching-to-learn activity.

At the Expo, we received several questions about what college courses are like, how one goes about getting into college, what kinds of things colleges teach, and what happens if you have difficulty and need help with the course work. With such naïve sounding questions, one might suspect they came from the children, but the parents asked these questions.

And, from the Cub Scouts, a recent communication addressed to the SCI 100 class said:

*We sure enjoyed our evening at the college with y'all. We all learned a lot and you gave us some thoughts about our own future plans. (You also helped us with our Scientist Badge.) Thank You.*

Whether it occurs between administrators and teachers, students and teachers, teachers and teachers, or students and students, collaboration is the key to any successful teaching program. Our teaching-to-learn experience promoted collaboration on all levels. Teachers can employ this effective instructional strategy in the classroom or in a service learning setting, and it is flexible enough to suit diverse goals. The outcomes go well beyond cognitive objectives and affect more than just the students involved. Teaching-to-learn makes a difference.

## References

Berliner, D. 1989. Being the teacher helps students learn. *Instructor* 98(9): 12–13.

Bonwell, C. C., and J. A. Eison. 1991. Active learning: Creating excitement in the classroom. ERIC Digest. ED340272.

Caprio, M. W. 1993a. Teaching seems more complicated than I first thought. *Journal of College Science Teaching* 22(4): 218–20.

Caprio, M. W. 1993b. Cooperative learning–The jewel among motivational-teaching techniques. *Journal of College Science Teaching* 22(5): 279–81.

Dewey, J. 1997.(Originally published in 1937). *Experience and Education.* New York: MacMillan Publishing Co.

McKeachie, W. J., P. R. Pintrich, Y. Lin, and D. A. Smith. 1986. Teaching and learning in the college classroom: A review of the research literature. ERIC Document. ED314 999.

NRC (National Research Council). 1996. *National Science Education Standards.* Washington, D.C.: National Academy Press.

Renkl, A. 1997, Learning by teaching. On the Internet at: *www.ph-gmuend.de/PHG/ phonline/Psychologie/ldl_engl.htm.*

Skinner, J. 1994. Learning by teaching. *Zielsprache Englisch* February:38–39.

Whitman, N. A. 1988. Peer teaching: To teach is to learn twice. *ASHE-ERIC Higher Education Report No. 4.* Washington, D.C.: Association for the Study of Higher Education. ERIC Identifier: ED 305 016.

Wiegand, D., and M. Strait. 2000. What is service learning. *Journal of Chemical Education* 77(12): 1538–1539.

Wlodkowski. R. J. 1985. *Enhancing Adult Motivation to Learn: A Guide to Improving Instruction and Increasing Learner Achievement.* San Francisco: Jossey-Bass Publishers.

# A Practical Application of Andragogical Theory Assumptions in Introductory Biology Courses

## Adopting an Educational Paradigm That Targets the Adult Learner

BRUNO BORSARI

As people mature, the critical elements affecting their education evolve to meet their changing needs and altering perspectives. According to Knowles (1980), the professional educator who is dealing with adult learners must be aware that an evolution must also occur from pedagogy (leading of the child) to andragogy (leading of the adult).

Indeed, modern educators of adults must become familiar with Knowles's paradigm if they wish to positively affect the educational experiences of their students. This paper will briefly describe the salient points of Knowles's andragological theory and will illustrate the efficacy of its application with a specific classroom example.

Knowles's theory describes four unique characteristics of adult learners. As people move toward adulthood:

- *Self-concept changes from dependency to self-directedness;*
- *A large reservoir of experience develops that can be a rich resource for learning;*
- *Readiness for learning is increasingly oriented toward helping them to cope in society;*
- *A perspective on education moves toward performance-centered learning with special interest in the application of knowledge.* (modified after Knowles, 1980)

The four critical elements of andragogy listed above are identical to the critical elements of pedagogy, but our assumptions about the child learner in relation to these elements are very different from those we hold for the adult learner. For example, child learners are more dependent on teacher-structured learning environments, their reservoir of experience is relatively insignificant as a major learning resource, they make fewer decisions about the courses they will take or curricula of interest, and their learning is content-centered.

Given the four assumptions about the characteristics of adult learners, college instructors can better understand the foundations of the psychological, emotional, and intellectual development of their students. The consideration of these principles and their application in everyday instruction should increase the learners' motivation and receptivity to the subject matter and ultimately promote student achievement.

Educators who are sensitive to this issue and are willing to apply these theoretical principles in adult learners' curricula will certainly succeed in increasing the effectiveness of their courses when adults are the recipients of the instructional effort.

## Instructional strategies for the adult learner

Facilitating adult learning can be a very complex process. It entails educators and learners bringing to an educational encounter varying personalities, different expectations, diverse learning styles, personal and professional experiences, and varied cultural and ethical backgrounds.

And, most importantly, "Cognitive psychologists and educators have come to recognize that effective instruction focuses on the active involvement of students in their own learning, with opportunities for teacher and peer interactions that engage students' natural curiosity" (Halpern and Associates 1994). New ways of learning emphasize questioning and cooperative group activities that keep students involved with the material they are learning. Learning rarely, if ever, occurs passively.

In 1975, Knowles developed the concept of inquiry teams to allow adult learners to fully participate in the educational encounter. This activity starts with the identification of learning needs and the translation of those needs into questions and learning objectives. Since then, numerous studies have been conducted on students' preferred learning styles (Dorsey and Pierson, 1984; Holtzclaw, 1985; Wilett and Adams, 1985; Conti

and Welborn, 1986; Korhonen and McCall, 1986). These studies emphasize the more pragmatic needs of the adult learner and confirm the andragological theory assumptions.

The College of St. Catherine, a private liberal arts college for women in St. Paul, Minnesota, successfully implemented the andragological educational theory in its biology classrooms. Norton et al. (1997) demonstrated that if scientific information is presented in a context of relevant social issues, rather than strictly as content, and if it relates to students' experiences as well as to other disciplines, students remain more interested and engaged in the learning process.

Another recent and remarkable study was conducted at Clemson University, a public land grant university in South Carolina, to determine individual differences in learning patterns among students enrolled in Clemson's general chemistry program. From these investigations it is clearly understood that "the student has some area/preference/ability in each type of functioning and can enhance those abilities by learning skills in those areas. The model does not attempt to determine or describe ability, but only preferences for types of action and interaction with people, things, and ideas" (Krause, 1998).

The increased enrollment of adult students in two-year colleges, in response to the demands of businesses seeking better skilled employees (Baker, 1996), is further evidence of the significance to adult learners of performance-based learning. Also important to adult students is the motivational value of a social context in which the learning occurs.

It appears, however, that instructors cannot effectively accommodate the students' educational needs without the students understanding their altered roles in the new classroom setting. These new roles imply a higher level of student cognition and maturity. Only through a shared understanding among learners and professors about the synergistic effect of the theory's basic principles can the practical aspects of the

**Figure 1.**

BIOLOGY EVALUATION FORM
STUDENT PRESENTATION SERIES

Presenter/s

Date:

Please take a few minutes at the end of this lecture to answer the questions below. Write your personal comments and give the speaker/s a score by circling one number on each question.

Thank you for your participation!

The speaker/s was/were well prepared and organized to deliver this lecture.

1  2   3   4   5   6   7   8   9   10

The main concepts of this lecture were effectively pointed out.

1  2   3   4   5   6   7   8   9   10

The use of visual materials helped me to better understand this presentation.

1   2   3   4   5   6   7   8   9   10

I have learned a lot from the presenters' lecture.

1   2   3   4   5   6   7   8   9   10

The speaker/s allowed enough time for questions and discussion.

1   2   3   4   5   6   7   8   9   10

Overall evaluation of the presentation.

Poor    Average    Good    Excellent

Comments:

understanding of classical biological phenomena. Unfortunately, many students are underprepared to meet this challenge in time to begin their college careers, and the nontraditional adult learners may have been out of school too long to have retained the necessary skills, if they ever had them.

Instructors must teach in one semester an enormous amount of content material on the introductory biology syllabi. In addition, classes are often too large (50 to 80 students per lecture section is not unusual) and time constraints become a critical factor in accommodating students' in-class and out-of-class educational needs. With all these impediments, it is not surprising that science courses on two-year campuses often experience high levels of attrition and generate student fear and dissatisfaction (Cowan and Piepgrass, 1997).

For these reasons, I decided to introduce an alternative learning activity in my introductory biology courses. I intended the activity to target primarily those students who were experiencing difficulties and were likely to eventually fail or drop out of the course; and the activity would speak to the basic assumptions of Knowles's andragological theory.

andragological theory be implemented. The professor's leadership and mentoring role seems to be an extremely important component for putting Knowles's theoretical assumptions into practice.

## An application of the theory

"Science teachers at two-year colleges know that anxiety in the classroom can be palpable in the initial days of the semester" (Cowan and Piepgrass, 1997). Many students feel overwhelmed in these courses in ways they have probably never experienced before in a classroom.

The vastness of the discipline of biology demands an adequate technical vocabulary and a specialized study methodology as well as a clear

The plan was to offer students at the beginning of the semester the opportunity to replace unsatisfactory test scores with scores earned by giving individual or group presentations on topics of their choice. The students arranged with me how and when to present their studies. The outcomes of their performances were measured on an appropriate form (**Figure 1**), filled out by both the student-audience and me at the end of each presentation.

I worked with four groups of students on this project. They were enrolled in introductory biology courses [BIOL.1001 (two sections), BIOL.1201, and BIOL.1002], which I taught from the fall semester of 1996 to the fall semester of 1997 at LSU Eunice. BIOL.1001 and BIOL.1002 are sequential courses for the nonmajor, and BIOL 1201 is an introductory offering for biology majors.

The evaluation form considered a core of five questions, each with a score ranging from one to 10. I added a sixth question to evaluate the overall competence of the presentations and encouraged students to write some personal comments at the bottom of the form. The final score was averaged from the students' scores and the instructor's score, so that the instructor had half the responsibility for the evaluation process. I weighted the evaluation procedure this way because of the larger critical mass of student-evaluators and to minimize student evaluations of presentations as outstanding simply because of his/her relationship to the presenter.

## Results

The results from this analysis indicate that student success can be achieved through oral presentations in biology courses. The data (**Table 1**) illustrate the positive outcome of student participation in class presentations. The scores obtained by all students who chose to take part in this experience demonstrate a remarkable level of achievement (**Table 2**) not always revealed by traditional testing practices.

The number of participating students and the number of presentations were limited (**Table 1**). The fact that only two presentations were given in BIOL.1201 (biology for science majors) may appear contradictory since the students in this class should have been highly motivated and particularly interested in the subject.

Reasonable explanations for this occurrence are varied. The one deserving more consideration has to do with the smaller number of difficulties the majors had with the subject matter. Their lack of interest in preparing for a presentation can be explained by their level of achievement as measured by traditional examinations, which were already commendable.

## Conclusion

This innovative modality of instruction was used, in part, to enhance students' educational responsibility. A college experience must also promote the freedom and the intellectual stimulation that encourage creativity. "A college education is a total experience that not only fosters intellectual growth but personal growth as well" (Newmann and Newmann, 1992).

During this activity, I observed enthusiasm, creativity, and personal thought in the students as they prepared for their presentations. Conti's and Welborn's point is well taken: "More is needed than the knowledge of a student's learning style in order to improve the quality of teaching and learning" (1986).

It is important to note that the positive outcome of this experiment was corroborated by course evaluation forms completed by the students at the end of each semester. But, based only on this simple investigation, it is difficult to make generalizations that could be applied to other courses and different educational environments.

Student presentations in introductory biology courses at LSU Eunice were an attempt to substantiate the andragological theory assumptions. This collaborative mode of instruction involving student participation also keeps sight of curriculum demands and tends to foster the greatest student achievement (Conti and

---

**Table 1.**
Student enrollment in biology courses at Louisiana State University-Eunice and participation in class presentations.

|  | Biology 1001 Fall 1996 | Biology 1201 Fall 1996 | Biology 1002 Spring 1997 | Biology 1001 Fall 1997 |
|---|---|---|---|---|
| Students enrolled | 50 | 45 | 81 | 51 |
| Students giving presentations | 10 | 3 | 15 | 15 |
| Presentations | 7 | 2 | 8 | 9 |

**Table 2.**
Descriptive statistical data relative to the scores of students' presentations.

|  | Biology 1001 Fall 1996 | Biology 1201 Fall 1996 | Biology 1002 Spring 1997 | Biology 1001 Fall 1997 |
|---|---|---|---|---|
| M | 89.35 | 88.33 | 78.13 | 84.93 |
| SD | 10.28 | 8.94 | 8.72 | 5.08 |
| Range | 71-100 | 78-93.5 | 70-92 | 80-98.5 |

---

Welborn, 1986). The student presentations generate discussion, arouse interest, and stimulate every one in the class. The independent study and research involved in preparing for a class presentation teaches students how to acquire scientific information and helps them to develop their communication skills in the subject area.

Norton said it this way: "The theme-based, investigative approach to teaching introductory biology offers faculty a way to emphasize the process of science over content. Students are excited by what they are learning and become actively involved in their own education" (Norton et al., 1997).

And, by facilitating this class activity, I improved my teaching skills by acquiring a better understanding of Knowles's andragological theory and the adult learners' educational needs.

**References**

Baker, G. A. III. 1996. Professors—Leaders within the community college movement. In *Graduate and Continuing Education for Community College Leaders: What It Means Today*, eds. J. C. Palmer and S. G. Katsinas, 77-86. San Francisco, CA: Jossey-Bass.

Conti, G. J., and R. B. Welborn. 1986. Teaching-learning styles and the adult learner. *Lifelong Learning* 9(8): 8-11.

Cowan, M. M., and K. W. Piepgrass. 1997. The first day of class on a two-year campus. *Journal of College Science Teaching* 27(2): 104-106.

Dorsey, O.L., and M.J. Pierson. 1984. A discriptive study of adult learning styles in a nontraditional education program. *Lifelong Learning: An Omnibus of Practice and Research* 7(8):8.

Halpern, D. F., and Associates, eds. 1994. *Changing College Classrooms. New Teaching and Learn-*

---

*ing Strategies for an Increasingly Complex World.* San Francisco: Jossey-Bass.

Holtzclaw, L. R. 1985. Adult learners' preferred learning styles, choice of courses, and subject areas for prior experiential learning credit. *Lifelong Learning* 8:23-27.

Knowles, M. S. 1975. *Self-Directed Learning: A Guide for Learners and Teachers.* Chicago: Follet.

Knowles, M. S. 1980. *The Modern Practice of Adult Education: From Pedagogy to Andragogy.* Cambridge Adult Education: Englewood Cliffs, N.J.

Korhonen, L. J., and R. J. McCall. 1986. The interaction of learning style and learning environment on adult achievement. *Lifelong Learning* 10(2): 21-23.

Krause, L. B. 1998. The cognitive profile model of learning styles: Differences in student achievement in general chemistry. *Journal of College Science Teaching* 28(1): 57-61.

Newmann, B. M., and P. R. Newmann. 1992. *When Kids Go to College. A Parent's Guide to Changing Relationships.* Columbus: Ohio State University Press.

Norton, C. G. et al. 1997. Reinvigorating introductory biology. A theme-based, investigative approach to teaching biology majors. *Journal of College Science Teaching* 27(2): 121-126.

# A Path Toward Integrated Science—The First Steps

## *Constructivist Teaching— Taking Small Steps to Reach Great Strides*

M. W. CAPRIO, PARRIS POWERS, JEFFERY D. KENT, SUSAN HARRIMAN, CHARLES SNELLING, PAULA HARRIS, AND MELISSA GUY

This semester Volunteer State Community College (VSCC) in Gallatin, Tennessee, took the first step to develop an integrated science course for its nonscience majors. That step, as part of VSCC's professional development program, consisted of organizing an interdisciplinary team to design the integrated course and a training program for those who would teach it.

The design team comprises five professors from the fields of chemistry, physics, mathematics, and biology. All are working together to teach a section of introductory biology for nonscience majors. The team selected a biology course as its training ground because of the inherent interdisciplinary nature of the subject.

All five instructors attend every class meeting. One of us (Caprio) delivers the lesson while the remaining instructors serve as master learners and work more closely with the students. The course is presented using a student-centered approach and it relies heavily on collaborative learning strategies.

We divided the class into four heterogenous groups of four or five students each and one master learner. The master learners learn along with and assist the students in their groups, but they do not evaluate the students. The five team instructors then meet weekly outside of class to discuss the progress of the biology course and the implications of the week's experience for the integrated science course they will be designing.

This column focuses on the progress over the first few weeks of this hothouse version of nonmajors' introductory biology (Bio100). (The course is in its seventh week of a fifteen-week semester.) To provide a more balanced picture, this article presents the views of the three different entities involved in the course: the instructor (Caprio), the master learners (Harriman, Kent, Powers, and Snelling), and two of the students (Guy and Harris).

### The instructor's view
*M. W. CAPRIO*
• *What were some early concerns?* This section of Bio100 was to be different in several important ways, and each variation brought with it some

risks. First, we were imposing an instructor's professional development program on a course for students. Running a professional development program concurrently with a real course, in real time, and with real students is certainly innovative, but that is only one element of the departure from traditionalism.

Bio100 typically meets for three hours of lecture and two hours of laboratory work a week. This section of Bio100, however, is scheduled in a laboratory room for two two-and-a-half-hour sessions each week. This arrangement lets me integrate hands-on activities into the course wherever appropriate and without regard to scheduling constraints. In addition, the larger time blocks allow us to incorporate local field trips into the class. Because I had to alter my pacing from the more familiar 75-minute lectures and two-hour laboratories to the new format, I also decided that the commercially available laboratory exercises needed significant revision. In the end, I decided to develop my own exercises.

A third change was the selection of the Biological Sciences Curriculum Study's new college program, *Biological Perspectives* (BSCS, 1998). This program is new for all of us. I chose it because it lends itself very well to a constructivist approach, it smooths the instructor's transition from traditional, encyclopedic books to a more conceptually based resource, and it is a necessary addition to a significantly different way of teaching biology to nonmajors.

Despite the departures from traditionalism, students enrolled in the course deserved the best class VSCC could offer. That would be the easy part. With five veteran instructors intent on creating a rich learning experience for them, these students' education would never be at risk.

• *What does it feel like?* The first two weeks were difficult because of a tension I felt between the professional development component of the course and the lessons I was presenting for the students. In my enthusiasm to showcase constructivism, I emphasized that approach excessively, which led me to disregard some of the necessary traditional methods I would have included had this been an ordinary semester without four other instructors in my classroom. Perhaps because I was the one standing at the front of the room, I assumed the responsibility for a professional development program that was really supposed to be a collaborative, independent learning experience for all five of the participants.

By the end of the second week, feedback from the students revealed that the strictly constructivist approach had not been working for them either, and a more balanced presentation was necessary. Professors sometimes forget that innovations in education are not only difficult for instructors to implement; students, too, are accustomed to traditional methods and are sometimes even more resistant to change than their teachers.

A more useful strategy was to develop sound lessons for the students, model effective teaching techniques that balanced constructivism and traditionalism, and discuss the strengths and weaknesses of each lesson in our weekly design team meetings. We would have felt so much more comfortable had we begun the course with the wisdom that came of our initial experiences.

• *How did it feel to be teaching a class with four of my colleagues present at every session, not as coinstructors but sitting with the students as master learners from whom I would be receiving feedback at our weekly meetings?* Well, it was—at first—a bit unnerving. No, it was, in fact, very unnerving. By the end of the second week, this level of self-consciousness was making me feel like it was impossible to survive the semester without extensive psychotherapy. It takes energy to maintain self-consciousness and sustain the illusion of perfection.

By the beginning of the third week no energy remained to preserve that fantasy and more forthright communication with the other members of the design team ensued. Now, rather than having four potentially critical colleagues observing me, I have four collaborators: the design team is beginning to function as a collaborative group and our professional development program is beginning to emerge as a collaborative learning experience for students and teachers alike.

The combined lab and lecture schedule has been easy to manage. For example, when lecturing about a microscopic structure it is natural to have students turn to their microscopes to observe it for themselves. Or, when talking about heart function, simply hand out stethoscopes and combine the rest of the lecture with direct experience. No science was ever done in a lecture hall, and to teach the whole course in a laboratory setting underscores the experiential nature of science for the students.

In student-centered teaching, a point is reached at which the teacher and the students come to understand their individual roles and realize that teaching and learning are not adversarial positions. The teacher comes to know that he or she facilitates, guides, and motivates; the students come to see that they can depend upon this kind of support from their teacher, although they are responsible for their own learning.

A bond of understanding develops whenever people work closely and well together, and the connection becomes stronger when the teaching and learning process operates properly. As this intellectual bond forms among the teachers and learners, a rich learning environment is created for everyone.

## The master learners

*PARRIS POWERS, JEFFERY D. KENT, SUSAN HARRIMAN, AND CHARLES SNELLING*

In a purely constructivist approach, we hold lecturing to a minimum and give students the resources and guidance to construct understanding of the subject. This hands-on, minds-on approach is slower and more frustrating to the students, who are more familiar with the traditional lecture setting. However, watching students grapple with the most fundamental concepts of science in this open-ended framework is giving us insight into how people learn.

For example, one of our first activities was having the students design and conduct a simple experiment. After giving out raisins and a clear, colorless carbonated beverage, Prof. Caprio asked the students to explain why the raisins alternately floated and sank in the beverage. From this, Prof. Caprio developed the basic physical concepts Socratically. He then asked the students to formulate a hypothesis and design experiments to discover a variable that would change the rate at which the raisins moved in the carbonated fluid.

As master learners, we assisted the students with the experiment, helped them discover how to use the equipment, and guided them as they developed their hypotheses and experimental protocols. It was hard not to interfere and show them *how* to solve the problem. As the activity progressed, the students used electronic balances, hydrometers, and thermometers, made measurements, and familiarized themselves with laboratory glassware. They discovered the concepts of Archimedes principle, density, specific gravity, and more. And, of course, they gained first-hand experience with the power of the scientific method. They also made a lot of mistakes.

Students can learn as much or more from their failures than they can from their successes, and in this setting there is time for students to process information and learn through their errors. But being *allowed* to make mistakes in school is not a familiar situation.

This approach is uncomfortable for students: it requires them to work constantly, to think critically, and—most importantly—to observe and reflect. Because of the sheer volume of material in traditional lecture courses, students do not always have the time to accomplish much real learning, and they frequently resort to rote memorization in place of developing these more substantial thinking and learning skills. Surely lectures can expose students to more material; but we must ask whether *more* is really *better* for them.

Prof. Caprio's approach was almost directly opposite what they experienced in other courses, which was disconcerting to them. In the early stages of the course, students were somewhat reticent and occasionally openly hostile to this approach. Much of this they said was due to their insecurity at not having a formal lecture where they would be responsible for a set amount of information. They perceived the course as not having enough structure, although, in fact, it is just structured differently. A great deal of students' uneasiness was likely due to their lack of familiarity with the teaching methods. Much of their concern may reflect a life-long exposure to fact-laden lecture presentations.

The design team's weekly meetings have been productive and have allowed us to evaluate questions and issues raised in the classroom. Through these discussions, our teaching approach has been redesigned slightly to give students a little more of the standard lecture to which they are accustomed. With that, they seem to be enjoying a firmer footing; they feel more in control and know better what is expected of them. The revised approach still asks them to stretch their comfort zones a bit, but now the stretch is easier for them to achieve.

The students now know how this approach differs from more traditional teaching and learning, and they see the advantages it offers. But their initial insecurities with the course were valid. A lesson learned by the instructor and master learners is that students are so committed to a fact-oriented, lecture-driven format that they resist change to a new learning strategy. In our zeal to embrace innovative teaching techniques, it is important to keep in mind that students need to be brought into the innovations at a reasonable pace that is comfortable for *them*.

Perhaps as the reform movement in science education progresses to the point where constructivist classrooms are more the rule than the exception, we may not need to be as attentive to this issue, but our experience in the first few weeks of this course tells us that time has not yet come.

We are impressed, and a little surprised, with the sense of loyalty shown by students and master learners in the collaborative groups established at the beginning of the semester. An undeniable bond has formed between all the group members, and the students in a group make a serious effort to help one another succeed. This responsibility to the group may be one of the factors contributing to the excellent attendance record of the students in this section. In general, the depth of the involvement and commitment of the faculty and students with each other and with the subject matter may be a primary effector for the success of this course.

### The students

*PAULA HARRIS AND MELISSA GUY*

In a standard biology course, students can work through material by memorizing names and structures without grasping concepts or interconnections.

Typical students find it possible to store many pieces of information in short-term memory, pass the required tests, go through the motions of the lab work, and emerge at the end of the semester with a passing grade, never having experienced eureka. But most of the factoids collected this way are lost within six months of the final exam. The constructivist approach, however, obligates students to work differently.

The constructivist format is enormously more challenging than the traditional method, although it may be a little heady for the student who needs to take a mandatory science course for a degree in another field. It was somewhat daunting at first to realize that we humanities and social science majors would have to learn to think as biologists to get through this course.

An objective of this method is to build understanding of the interrelated nature of all life instead of just learning about the puzzle pieces without grasping how to assemble them into a coherent picture. By placing the pieces in the

*With ample paper for lecture notes and a little caffeine to keep us alert, our class stepped into Bio100 expecting "science as usual." Just days into the course, however, we realized that we were not in a traditional biology class at all. We talked about the humanities, we learned about Galileo and Copernicus, and even Shakespeare was mentioned.*

*Initial interactions with fellow students were characterized by tension and a bit of confusion as we had four extra instructors in the classroom. It took some time before we realized that this course had been selected to be the "laboratory" for developing an integrated science course for nonscience majors. We were part of an experiment!*

*With instructors all with different science backgrounds collaborating and working beside us as master learners, a scholarly atmosphere has developed. Traditional lectures have been replaced by open discussions and the learning process is enriched by a variety of experiences, including hands-on lab work and field trips.*

*We are receiving a very comprehensive view of science. For me, science has been redefined. It is no longer white lab coats, hi-tech jargon, and exclusive knowledge. We are discovering the correlation between science and the humanities and have begun to consider practical applications. The scientific method has become a real learning tool as we have gathered information and made hypotheses. I didn't know science could be this interesting!*

*In addition to a new-found interest in the sciences, I have been personally transformed by the innovative teaching and learning style. As an education major, I have been particularly impressed with the way Prof. Caprio introduces material, with the technique of group learning while being "coached" by a master learner, and with the process of actively, methodically pursuing knowledge. This has been quite a contrast to most of my classroom experiences, which have involved the traditional transfer of knowledge: the instructor talks, the class listens.*

*In conclusion, I am looking forward to the remainder of this course. I can say without reservation that I have been schooled and that this learning experience has given a new perspective to a future educator.*

*—Melissa Guy*

context of the life process, students gain a sense of wonder and understanding of the whole. The appreciation of the splendid linkages interacting in homeostasis is an example where knowing the individual parts, even in minute detail, means much less to the nonscientist than even a general concept of the whole.

Getting to that level of knowing is hard work. However, an important function of a college education is to help us students grow to become more than we were before, and that means we must do more than before. There is something personal about information you discover for yourself, maybe because we value things more when we invest ourselves in acquiring them.

What do we like best about this format? That would probably be the sense of camaraderie and mutual respect among teachers and students. Once we got over our initial panic, we students came to see ourselves as scientists.

Why did we experience the panic? Perhaps because it is hard to shed habits and expectations formed in more than twelve years of traditional classrooms. It takes a few weeks to develop faith in the system and faith in yourself as a member of the team. What we like least is that this section of Bio100 is regarded as comparable to the standard course.

Because of its teaching/learning method, the course catalog should differentiate this section from the traditionally taught Bio100 course. This course requires much more work than typical ingest-and-regurgitate classes, and that distinction should be accorded recognition.

Of the 19 students who enrolled in this course, 15 prefered the constructivist method to the traditional approach. All students said they would be more comfortable with this approach if the instructor would provide more basic information (e.g., definitions and general concepts) in a lecture to orient them as new chapters are introduced. The impression is that the material is slanted toward a more scientifically literate student body although the course is posted as introductory.

A second, double-edged issue concerns meeting time that is required outside of class. One drawback is that it is hard to schedule out-of-class meetings for group projects, and this course involves many such meetings. The up side of this requirement is that we are learning to look beyond the lectures and textbooks for information and to work interdependently.

Finally, the unanimous consensus was that a student who completes this Bio100 course will retain significantly more information than if that same student had taken a traditionally structured section of the course. If this style offers students more concepts but fewer facts, it is still advantageous because subject matter that is *understood* stays with us longer than myriad unrelated data. And by the time we have searched, suffered, and speculated together, we really *do* understand the subject.

## Final remarks from the instructor

I do not wish to analyze the information that my colleagues and students have presented here for you. I also do not want to force my conclusions on you, but I need to be certain we have not misinformed you. The master learner's section of this article implies that constructivism equates with a lack of structure. This is not true. The structure in a constructivist classroom is different, but it does exist. My teaching style—regardless of the approach I use—does tend to be loosely structured. It is important that a personal characteristic of one teacher not be misassigned as a feature of constructivism.

Of a similar nature, one of the students in this article remarks that the course content is slanted toward more scientifically literate students. For better or worse, part of my approach is to try to gauge the students' level as soon as possible and to pitch my presentations within reach, but just a little above their grasp.

### Reference

BSCS. 1998. *Biological Perspectives*. Dubuque, IA: Kendall/Hunt Publishing Company.

# Are We Cultivating 'Couch Potatoes' in Our College Science Lectures?

## Weeding Out the Bad Teaching Habits That Inhibit Students' Growth

THOMAS R. LORD

At a recent annual meeting of marketing executives in New York City, the nationally known keynote speaker announced to the audience that *couch potato* television watchers outnumber their *noncouch potato* counterparts by almost two to one.

To earn the distinction of being a couch potato, the speaker continued, two things were necessary. First, a couch potato candidate had to watch more than 25 hours of TV a week (an amount reached by over 78 percent of the American public). More importantly, during the time the viewer is watching television, his or her attention to specifics can be no more than 50 percent of his or her capacity.

The speaker's reason for providing the information was to make the point that, in today's highly competitive commercial marketplace, promotional advertising need not be overly detailed to convince consumers to purchase the product. Sometimes I feel today's students are more like couch potatoes than ardent learners. I recall visiting a colleague who, several years earlier, had left my college to take a position at a large re-

search university. I arrived at his institution just as his mid-morning general biology class was about to begin. Noting the time, he invited me to take a seat in the back of the lecture hall to "soak in" his lecture. I decided to take him up on his invitation and found an empty chair in the center of the last row of the theater.

As I sat there, the hall quickly filled with undergraduates. I was struck by the fact that most of the students seemed semi-awake as they moved toward the same swing-out arm chairs they had taken since the first day of class. Once seated, they pulled tattered notebooks from their unzipped backpacks and stationed them on their desks. With notebooks in place, the students comfortably waited for the lecture to begin.

As my friend was about to speak, a few students entered the room more lethargic then their classmates and maneuvered in my direction to the back of the lecture hall. There they lowered themselves into the few remaining unoccupied seats, skipped the backpack part of the ritual, and awaited the professor's opening words.

By then my colleague was in place behind a lectern and next to a large chalkboard in the front of the hall. As he began his lecture I could hear the scrawl of pencils and the whirl of paper as students prepared to take notes. Besides these sounds and the jawing gum-chewers in front of me, the presenter's voice was the only other sound in the room. The students dutifully sat scribbling notes onto their pads: no one disrupted the presentation, no one raised a hand, and no one questioned their role in the learning process. About 20 minutes into the lecture the mood was interrupted when the teacher interjected a humorous, personal experience into his presentation. The event redirected the class's focus from the notebooks to the professor, and mild laughter and talking arose from the gallery. For a few short minutes, my colleague had regained the students' attention, but it was short-lived, and the atmosphere quickly returned to the previous quiet as he returned to his prescriptive delivery.

Forty minutes into the lecture I looked around the room: a handful of kids were still frantically taking notes, several students were copying the terms that the professor had earlier written on the chalkboard, and a few were sleeping or reading the college newspaper, but most of the students were just sitting quietly. Despite their opened eyes, their stares were unfocused and their faces held no expression. These students reminded me of the passive couch potatoes the marketing conference speaker had described.

The students remained that way for a while longer when suddenly the activity level picked up in the room. The eyes of the students refocused as they took control of their postures, and I immediately realized the reason for the change. My colleague had asked if there were any questions about what he had presented during the hour. Despite their now attentive frame of mind, no questions were raised by the audience and the class ended. Students stuffed their pencils and notebooks into their backpacks, grabbed their jackets, and moved out of the lecture hall.

I got up, and walked to the front to join my friend as he stuffed the last page of his lecture into his attaché case. Noticing me approach, he asked if I'd like to join him for a lunch at his ex-

pense. Since I never turn down an invitation for a free meal, we adjourned to the faculty dining room of the university.

Over lunch, my friend conveyed how proud he was of the modifications he had made with the course I had witnessed. During the previous summer he had spent several weeks adding new, cutting-edge findings to every course topic and had (in his words) "brought the course up to the twenty-first century." Then, with a inquisitive expression on his face, he asked what I thought of the class I had just seen.

A long time went by before I answered. I didn't want to tell him that his students didn't pay much attention during the lecture and that they probably didn't learn a great deal, but I couldn't tell him what he expected to hear either. "I'm sorry Jack, what did you say?" I asked, stalling for time and hoping something would come to me.

"What did you think of my lecture?" he reiterated. Again it seemed like minutes passed as my mind searched for a response. Nothing came to me, but I realized that I had to answer his question: "You're sure giving your students a challenging science course," I blurted and congratulated him on his grasp of the difficult content. Before he could respond, I quickly added, "What do you think of this university's fringe benefit package?" I managed to avoid discussing my colleague's teaching for the rest of my visit.

As I drove back to my college later that day, I wondered why science professors are so reluctant to give up the old lecture method of teaching. Surely professors who follow the practice realize that, despite their attendance, the students aren't putting much effort into the learning process. And when the students *are* listening, most of them are too busy scribbling notes to think about the substance of the lecture.

Another friend, who teaches at a university in Great Britain, jokingly refers to this common practice in American higher education as the "sponge and liquid" principle of teaching. "Every time an American professor enters the class," he would say, "he carries with him a pouch full of irrefutable content as if it were some kind of astute liquid. During the delivery, the professor casts the liquid throughout the lecture hall, sometimes in sprinkles and other times in torrents. As this happens, sponges (the students) roll about the room in an attempt to absorb as much of the liquid as they possibly can before it evaporates (I wish my students were as active). But the sponges are not all the same."

My English friend added, "[The sponges] are of different shapes, sizes, and absorptive potentials. Large, pliable sponges have an easier time of soaking up the liquid than small, pliable sponges, but quickly moving small sponges can soak up more liquid than slow moving large ones. So there is not only the problem of acquiring the critical information before it evaporates, but there's the complication of all the other sponges getting in the way."

"The continuous and constant competition for the information," continued my British colleague, "creates a learning environment that is neither healthy nor supportive. By mid-term, most of the sponges (especially those that find the fluid distasteful anyway) give up rolling in the liquid and exert only enough effort to remain moist until the course ends. Furthermore, many of the sponges suited for this method of teaching also tire of the competition and join their dampened companions."

Many science professors consider "sponge and liquid" lecturing to be the only way to teach at the college level. After all, lecturing does let the students know exactly what the professor thinks is important and what will likely appear on the exams. Lecturing seems to be the easiest way to teach science; it's easily adapted to different audiences and time frames, and it allows the professor to constantly remain the focus of the class.

I wondered if lecturing in science really could do more harm than good to student learning. The more I thought about it, the more convinced I became that it could, for these reasons:

- Lecturing is based on the assumption that all college students have the same level of background knowledge on the science topic. Lectures can waste the better students' time by covering things that they already know or can easily read for themselves. Lectures for the weaker student, however, usually brings on frustration and disinterest (Brown et al., 1989).
- Science lectures are always given at the same pace. Educational theorists tell us, however, that college students learn science at a variety of paces; some are very quick at grasping concepts while others need time to mull over the content before they understand it (Kulik and Kulik, 1979).
- Science lectures are always presented verbally despite the fact that many of today's students are either strong visual learners or are heavily dependent on manipulatives or other hands-on exploratory activities for their learning (Johnson et al., 1991).
- Most college students don't feel comfortable asking questions during lectures and exit the class with misconceptions and incorrect understandings that they have not identified (Stone, 1970; Bowers, 1986).
- And, finally, the level of scientific knowledge gained by students from lectures tends to be low-level, factual content and not the high-level critical thinking and problem solving forms of learning sought in higher education (Bligh, 1997; Gabbert et al., 1986; Ruggiero, 1988).

But what could science instructors use to replace the lecture? Professors just can't show video movies or assign readings each time students gather for class. As I continued to drive, I continued to think about this when a highway billboard caught my attention. The sign showed a cluster of young adults in thoughtful pose around a small table. In the hand of each person was a bottle of chilled beer while on the table small pine blocks were strewn around a complicated wooden puzzle. The boldface message proclaimed: PENNSY BEER, FOUND WHERE IMPORTANT DISCOVERIES IN LIFE ARE BEING MADE.

As I read the sign I thought about how people discover and learn in real life and quickly concluded that most folks learn through inquiry, basing the new understandings on what they already know. Sometimes they're able to do this without help, but most of the time men and women collaborate with their friends and co-workers. People learn as they try to figure out questions, puzzles, statements, and other challenges. They launch new learning from their existing knowledge base and can usually be most successful at doing so by collaborating with others.

Instructors, therefore, shouldn't lecture students to supply them with facts to memorize and store for later reference. Instead, the professor's job is to provide challenging experiences and problems that students try to solve based on what they already know. As they figure things out, they learn and build higher levels of knowledge in their minds.

Rather than finding the solution in their textbook or study guide, students should be encouraged to develop their own solutions based on questions the teacher provides. In addition, instructors need to give students the chance to discuss with others and incorporate new understandings and insights. Professors shouldn't *cover the content* for their students; rather, they should *uncover* it.

As my drive home ended, I pulled into a parking lot at my college and found that I had convinced myself that I needed to change my way of teaching science. I knew my students were not learning as much as they could. I knew I could be a more effective teacher and better instill a respect for science in my students. But most of all, I knew I could no longer continue to give my teacher-centered lectures and cultivate couch potatoes in my classes.

### References

Bligh, D. A. 1997. *What's the Use of Lectures.* Harmondsworth, England: Penguin.

Bowers, J. 1986. Classroom communication apprehension. *Communication Education* 35(4): 372-378.

Brown, J., A. Collins, and P. Duguid. 1989. Situated cognition and the culture of learning. *Educational Researcher* 18(1): 32-42.

Gabbert, B., D. Johnson, and R. Johnson. 1986. Cooperative learning, groups-to-individual transfer, process gain and the acquisition of cognitive reasoning strategies. *Journal of Psychology* 120(3): 265-278.

Johnson, D., R. Johnson, and K. Smith. 1991. *Active Learning: Cooperation in the College Classroom.* Edina, MN: Interaction Book Company.

Kulik, J., and C. Kulik. 1979. College teaching. In *Research on Teaching: Concepts, Findings and Implications,* eds. P.L. Peterson and H.J. Walberg. Berkeley, CA: McCutcheon.

McKeachie W. 1988. Teaching thinking. *Update* 2(1): 1.

Ruggiero, V. 1988. *Teaching Thinking Across the Curriculum.* New York: Harper & Row.

Stone, E. 1970. Students' attitudes to the size of teaching groups. *Educational Review* 21(2): 98-108.

# Chaos and Opportunity

*Minimizing Obstacles Along the
Track to the Constructivist
Approach*

M. W. CAPRIO

I n its most recent monograph (1997), the Society for College Science Teachers (SCST) explored problems that arise as teachers move from traditional methods toward innovative ones. As I look back at the monograph, I see the problems the authors described as falling into four distinct classes: administrative conflicts, logistical problems, friction in peer relationships, and student-related concerns.

Organizing the obstacles classroom innovators face into discrete categories may help us to address them in a more systematic way and ultimately facilitate our search for solutions.

Conflict with administrative expectations is a particularly frustrating category of problems facing innovators, especially when the administration is mired in traditionalism and the faculty member has read the literature, listened carefully at meetings of the National Science Teachers Association, and is willing and able to make the reform effort.

Brilliant teachers who are practicing cutting-edge classroom approaches have been denied tenure or promotion because of supervisors who are unable to appreciate the quality of the faculty member's work. Fortunately, this bias is easing as the reform effort is taking hold across more of our nation's campuses.

Primary among the logistical problems is the issue of class size. While it certainly is possible to adapt student-centered approaches to large lecture settings, small classes clearly offer a much more friendly environment for these approaches. Although somewhat less significant than class size, logistical obstacles also include such issues as classroom design, furniture placement, whether the chairs are moveable, and if there are tables at which collaborative groups can work comfortably.

A third class of difficulties arises from intradepartmental chaffing between the traditionalists and the innovators, which can, in extreme cases, give an academic department a split personality (to the extent that departments can have personalities). Change is—to some degree—difficult for everyone, but education tends to be one of the more conservative enterprises, and we would expect to find resistance to change within its ranks.

Modeling good teaching and letting the results speak for the process do not always set new directions. Indeed, sometimes innovation is suspect. And those who espouse change are not always held in high regard by their more traditional colleagues.

Modeling change may be the only real way to make progress, but challenging the cozy comfort of our colleagues' status quo has never been a very good way to win friends. Junior faculty are particularly vulnerable: Color outside the lines and surely a grownup will try to take your crayons away.

Finally, there are problems that arise from the expectations and past experiences of education's primary stakeholders, the students. One would presume that youth would welcome the new and different: young people have often been characterized as willing to flock to the latest fads without question. It is at once refreshing and daunting that when it comes to their classroom experiences, they are often more wary and conservative than we might expect (Zoller, 1997, 7).

In this column, there is only enough space to consider one of these four categories. The last of the problem classes listed above, the student-related issues, is the topic I will address here, looking at two specific matters within the category. One matter has to do with the implications and management of the new student/teacher relationship that develops when the teacher moves from behind the podium to work more closely with the students. The other pertains to the difficulties that can arise in the student-centered classroom when the students do not have the requisite social skills for successful collaborative work.

## A new student/teacher relationship

Instructors traditionally dispense information that students must absorb. Then the students show they have "learned" a topic by regurgitating it on examinations. The lecture serves primarily to demonstrate to students what sort of intellectual behavior they will have to emulate on exams. Generally speaking, students can do well in these kinds of courses and exams and are comfortable with them.

We now know, however, that the traditional model of teaching and learning does not help students convert information into knowledge. That is, it does not facilitate the incorporation of new information into the students' existing cognitive frameworks in ways that link it to pre-

existing knowledge and promote its retention (Meyers and Jones, 1993; McKeachie, 1986).

The traditional classroom is an important comfort zone for many teachers and students, but when we seek to help our students construct knowledge, and not merely collect information, we must keep in mind that people only "...make knowledge as part of a community of practice in which [they] do things together and talk about what they do" (Brent, 1996). The shift from classroom passivity to activity that is required to construct knowledge is discomforting for some. Then, too, Brent tells us:

> Learning occurs at the point where students are in a little over their heads, where conceptual gaps open and create problems that can only be solved by applying new knowledge and new forms of thinking which must be constructed for the occasion. The gap creates the occasion for the conversations that fill it. Our role is to be part of those conversations, providing modeling and guidance, letting students pick our brains when they find that there are things which they need to pick them for. (1996)

Here the teacher is seen as a resource and a coach, but clearly the responsibility for driving and shaping the learning is shifted from the teacher to the student. Such a shift portends an inevitable shift in the student/teacher relationship.

No matter how helpful that coach is, it is abundantly clear to the students that it is that formerly *very* helpful instructor who has deliberately stepped away from her "rightful" place behind the podium to create this unusually challenging learning environment. And, yes, students sometimes do get angry. Mostly, though, they are not as angry as they are frightened and frustrated. Because students are responsible for shaping their own learning, they are less clear about what the teacher expects from them in this new learning environment. They are often afraid that this new approach may destroy their grade point average (Caprio et al., 1998). This is not an uncommon student response; it seems to happen every semester in student-centered classes, and experienced instructors can sense it coming.

What can we say or do to avoid, minimize, or reverse students' worries about the constructivist approach? The answer is surprisingly simple: students need us to address just two points. First, the students want assurance that they will not be underevaluated in the course (get poor grades) because of *our* teaching methods. And second, albeit a less pressing concern for most, students want to know that they are getting a good education even if it is a different type of education than they expected it to be.

What their teacher's response needs to be is almost too obvious to say. First, we need to provide assessment feedback early and often. When we regularly grade and return quizzes, short papers, and homework projects, students will have a chance to see that their performance in the different setting is not too different from that which they have come to expect of themselves in general, and it may even be better. On the other hand, giving weak and infrequent feedback to the students fails to address their concerns and will result in losing them unnecessarily.

How can we assure students that constructivism is sound education? On the first day of class when most of us are introducing the course and reviewing the course outline, we can take a few minutes to summarize the educational literature that supports the student-centered approach. When I do this, I find I need to remind them about it again after a few weeks, when the semester's tensions begin to increase. Students can be partners in the teaching and learning process, and most of them will enthusiastically subscribe to the innovative pedagogies if they understand that it is in their best interest and is soundly based.

I have a story to tell that is germane to this point. After a 10-minute lecture vignette during which students received the basic information required to solve the problem, I gave them models of a four-chambered heart and charged them with determining the scheme of circulation (a different approach, perhaps, but a classic topic in introductory biology courses).

"No reference materials allowed except for the models and everything in your heads. There will be a quiz on this topic in 20 minutes. I'm here to help if you need me," I said.

After the students worked for about three minutes one of them asked, "Hey, Mario, why don't you just tell us the answer so we can learn it?"

I raised my eyebrows. "Hmm?" I said, trying to appear somewhere between not quite understanding the question and not seeing the reason for it. Almost immediately, though, the answer came from another student: "He's just trying to make us think; it's that constructivist thing."

Students have a vested interest in the educational process. When they understand that process—its mechanism, goals, and objectives—they become our colleagues in the classroom. Developing and strengthening student/teacher relationships empowers all the players in the teaching and learning system (Sorcinelli, 1996).

## Skills for collaboration

Utilizing collaborative groups is a powerful teaching and learning technique. But for students whose education has been individualistic and competitive, collaboration requires social skills that may still be relatively underdeveloped. Simply throwing students together and giving them a problem on which to work does not guarantee that any useful collaboration will occur.

Just as it is useful for students who will be working in a constructivist classroom to know at least a little about constructivism, it is equally important for students who will be working in collaborative groups to know some of what contributes to group success. Students also need to learn about how to maximize the experience for their own growth in the subject matter as well as for their personal development as effective group members.

One approach to addressing this problem is to invite a social scientist to discuss the dynamics of group work with the students. To differing degrees, most of us—their science teachers—have worked as group members at one time or another. We can try to impart what we've learned about group dynamics to our students, but learning to be part of an effective group is an important skill, and it may not be one that should be taught to our students by amateurs (us).

One of the advantages that comprehensive community colleges offer is a cadre of instructional specialists who are very willing to bring their expertise to bear on our students. We rely on librarians to help us teach the rudiments of information literacy and reading specialists to help us select appropriate texts and then show students how to work with those books. We also send students to the math lab when they are having problems with quantitative issues and to the writing center to learn how to write better.

Although we may not always maximize its value, teachers are really part of what can be a very powerful instructional team. Adding a psychologist or sociologist to that team will bring it the knowledge and talent to support student groups.

Such a discussion of group work with students might include a list of some of the characteristics that contribute to the success of groups. Some of the more frequently cited of those characteristics include the following (SEDL, 1994; Sowell, 1999):

- *There are well-defined group goals*: The group is working to produce a particular product and all the members understand what that product is to be.
- *The group has a plan*: The members agree on a strategy for achieving their goals.
- *Individual accountability exists*: Each member has a unique assignment that interrelates with the tasks of the other members and contributes to the strategic plan.
- *The group is interdependent*: Members are sharing knowledge, ideas, and strategies for success.

- *There is trust among group members*: Members are willing to take risks and admit their weaknesses.

From the start, some groups will be emotionally and intellectually better equipped to succeed than others, but knowing about the elements for success will help all of them to be more introspective about the collaborative process. And, once the teacher is aware of these attributes for group success, she can work individually or with a social scientist to enhance them in groups that may be faltering.

## Conclusion

"The Chinese use the same character, *wei ji*, for the words *chaos* and *opportunity*. This character would aptly describe the climate and crisis in science education in the United States during the 1970s and 1980s" (Chang, Undated).

The differences between the traditional teacher-centered approach and the more innovative student-centered techniques do open the possibility for chaos, but new opportunities are created, too. We must adjust to an altered student/teacher relationship, but the change brings the rewards of a more collegial classroom environment and a significant gain in the construction of knowledge.

The implementation of collaborative techniques requires that we go outside our disciplines to learn more about group dynamics, but that search only enriches the learning environment and enhances students' social development. In fact, it seems that these things we started out calling *problems* have been cleverly concealing important *opportunities* for growth of our students, our profession, and ourselves.

### References

Brent, D. 1996. Knowledge received/knowledge constructed: Principles of active learning in the disciplines. A keynote address presented at the Teaching and Learning and Writing Across the Curriculum Faculty Development Workshop, Laurentian University.

Caprio, M. W., ed. 1997. *From Traditional Approaches Toward Innovation.* Greenville, SC: Society for College Science Teachers.

Caprio, M. W., P. Powers, J. D. Kent, S. Harriman, C. Snelling, P. Harris, and M. Guy. 1998. A path toward integrated science: The first steps. *Journal of College Science Teaching* 27(6): 430-434.

Chang, Amy L. Undated. *The Origins of CELS.* Internet: *www.wisc.edu/cbe/cels/monograph/mono6x06.htm.*

Meyers, C., and T. B. Jones. 1993. *Promoting Active Learning: Strategies for the College Classroom.* San Francisco: Jossey-Bass.

McKeachie, W. J. 1986. *Teaching Tips: A Guidebook for the Beginning College Teacher.* Lexington, MA: Heath.

SEDL. 1994. Cooperative learning. *Classroom Compass* 1(Fall): 2.

Sorcinelli, Mary D. 1996 Assoc. Provost for Teaching, University of Massachusetts, Amherst, MA. Personal communication.

Sowell, K. 1999. Counseling and Testing Services, Volunteer State Community College, Gallatin, TN. Personal communication.

Zoller, U. 1997. The traditional-to-innovative switch in college science teaching: An illustrative case study on the reform trail. In *From Traditional Approaches Toward Innovation*, ed. M. W. Caprio. Greenville, SC: Society for College Science Teachers.

# Getting There from Here

*Making the Transition from
Traditional Teaching Practices to
Those That Are Student Centered*

M. W. CAPRIO AND LYNDA B. MICIKAS

An often-told story begins with a confused traveler stopping to ask for directions from a wise old farmer with a wry sense of humor. The motorist has wandered into the back country of one state or another—the story appears in many versions—having exhausted all possibilities of self-help. As expected, the traveler is entirely at the mercy of the local expert.

The farmer clearly knows of the traveler's desired destination and, at first, seems able to direct him there. He begins to give the directions. However, each time he stops part way through, abandons the explanation, and begins anew. Finally, after several false starts, he removes his straw hat, wipes his brow, and scratches his head pensively. He has confused even himself. Then he looks into the eyes of the stranger for a moment, shakes his head slowly, and with a very serious expression, says, "Well, come to think of it, my friend, you just can't get there from here."

When the confused traveler is a college science teacher moving from traditional teaching practices to active learning methods in education, a point frequently arrives in the transition when it seems that "you just can't get there from here." The reality, however, is that others have already made the journey and they have brought back some excellent directions.

Moving from a lecture format to one that is more student centered is a difficult step, and there are several reasons for the reluctance invariably felt by teachers who are contemplating the move. The barriers seem to come in two forms. First, there is the "why-should-I?" obstacle. This is the most basic hurdle to reform and arises from the view that we are, after all, good lecturers; we enjoy lecturing, our students pass courses when we lecture at them, and we have all those wonderful "class-tested" lecture notes. So why change? We offer a nonstandard answer to that question below.

Second, there is the "why-I-should-not" obstacle. This barrier to reform is more complex than the first and includes a whole set of reasons that range from excuses in the name of coverage and logistics to very real concerns. We discuss this second barrier to reform in the next section.

## Why should I go there

Why should one change to more student-centered approaches for teaching introductory college science courses? Sound educational reasons exist to explain why, and pedagogues are out in droves proclaiming them to the masses. Indeed, it would be difficult—perhaps impossible—to attend a meeting of science teachers without hearing educational researchers celebrate the new methods and urge their adoption in classrooms.

Their explanations are the standard responses to the question of *why change?*, and you can read about them in literature (Caprio, 1994; Leonard, 1997; Lord, 1996; Halyard, 1993; Yager, 1991).

But what we promised you here were less conventional reasons, of which we offer two. They are also important, and together with the pedagogical support for reform, they make a compelling case for change.

The first reason is simply that student-centered teaching is fun. Students find it fun, as do teachers. For the teacher, one kind of fun comes in the satisfaction of seeing learning in action. During lectures, we deliver the material, but students learn it elsewhere, in our absence. Of course, that happens when we use active teaching and learning strategies, too. Now, however, teachers have daily opportunities to see their students become involved with the course material, with each other, and with them. The excitement of learning is very evident during these interactions. Teachers find themselves smiling a lot as their students discover the subject matter and construct its meaning for themselves. When we work this way with our students we really feel we are teaching, because we witness learning happening directly before us and we know we play a role in catalyzing it. This is enormously satisfying and rather fun, too.

Student-centered teaching brings with it another kind of fun. Educators often describe lecturing as a passive experience for students. But in the words "for students" is implied an active experience for instructors. We are not entirely sure of that. The instructor does prepare the lecture, which involves interaction with the subject matter. In the classroom, however, the teacher is not working with the ideas of science so much as practicing public speaking, while students are mostly engaged in transcription. Sad to say, but in the time they spend together, neither is doing much thinking about science, except in a superficial way. Switch to an active learning strategy, though, and all that changes. Now both instructor and students are grappling with the ideas of

science together. They are thinking and asking questions. They are talking about science with one another and with the teacher. And that really is fun.

Perhaps it is not very scholarly to suggest "fun" as a reason for using a particular approach to teaching. But to not seek ways to bring the excitement and pleasure of discussing science to one's classroom is to belie the very reason we chose to do and teach science. We picked the profession because we enjoy teaching. If we fail to offer opportunities for our students to experience this type of pleasure, we conceal from them the power of science to realize intellectual fulfillment. In fact, using student-centered strategies—capitalizing on the fun of thinking and talking about science—allows us to more easily address the difficult domain of effective teaching goals, yet another argument for lecturing less.

A second reason for using student-centered teaching strategies is that these approaches make students partners in the teaching and learning processes. These strategies involve more students, more frequently and more deeply, in the process of learning. *All* students, not just the few who normally contribute to class discussions, participate in class, at a deeper level and more successfully. In fact, we have never seen a student fall asleep during an active learning session (one of us has actually heard a student snoring during what was a truly magnificent lecture), and class attendance is noticeably better. Transcription can happen whether a student attends class or not; learning, when the central result of having poured over the course content with other students and the instructor, cannot take place if a student is absent. Students quickly figure this out, and come to class because there is no easy substitute for what they gain by being present.

Acknowledging that students are partners in the teaching and learning process may also yield other rewards. The ultimate responsibility for learning has always resided with the students; if the students do not master the coursework, they and not the teacher suffer the consequences. This is implicit in all college courses. Student-centered approaches make the students' responsibility explicit and provide them with the tools, resources, and support they need to meet that responsibility. In this learning environment, they also have the opportunity to employ learning models similar to the ones used in the working world, where the responsibility for learning rests clearly on the individual.

## Why I should not go there

The case for active learning strategies—the answer to the "why-should-I" obstacle—is so strong that only the most formidable barrier could prohibit its acceptance. But for many of us, another important impediment exists: the various reasons each of us can give for "why I should not." We must identify these reasons and distinguish the real ones from those with less substance.

Of the latter (with the risk of alienating a few readers, we can call them *excuses*), we hear two most often. The first is the concern that active learning strategies make it impossible to "cover" the content listed in the syllabus. In fact, actual classroom experience and rigorous educational research has disproved this argument (Caprio, 1994; Bonwell and Eison, 1991). Many active learning strategies are comparable to lectures in promoting mastery of content. They are even superior to lectures in promoting the development of students' thinking, speaking, and writing skills. Once students develop these important learning skills, they can assume more responsibility for learning content on their own.

The second excuse claims that these methods are not appropriate for large classes. However, many ways exist to bring effective active learning experiences into a large lecture hall. Consider, for example, this passage from a recent monograph published by the Society for College Science Teachers:

> Most of my teaching is, as it was, in huge rooms with hundreds of students in them. (Sigh.) But my teaching strategies have ex-

panded way beyond the lecture. This past semester I conducted 340 students who have performed their own symphony of science. We did hands-on, "laboratory" exercises, in a room that holds 400 people sitting in chairs bolted to the floor. Architects designed those rooms for lecturing, but you can turn them into other kinds of teaching spaces. One day groups of my students were blowing up balloons in order to understand how the universe expands. Another day, they were dunking plastic drink bottles in baggies filled with ice to explore the dependence of temperature on pressure. (Shipman, 1997)

Peter Frederick (1987) describes five areas where active learning can occur in large classes. Other "why-I-should-not" concerns, which are very real, might if unaddressed, lead us to *reject* the arguments for using student-centered strategies in our classrooms. These concerns have one very important element in common: they all evolve from our commitment to offer our best to our students. None of us wants to provide less than our best effort, and if we lecture well, it seems risky to abandon that approach for new techniques with which we feel less secure.

So how do we handle these concerns? One approach is simply to look at them carefully. If we can better understand them, we might be able to find reasonable ways around them. We discuss two potential and closely related concerns below, and then consider some ways to "get there from here," these problems notwithstanding.

One concern, not often expressed by faculty but perhaps often felt, is that *in a traditional lecture, the lecturer controls virtually everything about the class meeting.* For the most part, this is how it was when we were students. We sat in lecture sections where, in addition to science, we learned about teaching. Our professors were our models. So when we were deciding whether to pursue teaching careers, we matched our personalities against our teachers, and when we started to teach, theirs was the model we emulated.

In addition, we expected teaching to put us in control at the "head of the class" when we signed our first teaching contracts. We were comfortable with that role; it is a secure position to hold. It is secure because we know how to make things work when we lecture and how to respond when the unexpected happens. We know we can look and feel successful with this approach. Now, though, someone is suggesting that we switch from a teacher-centered to a student-centered classroom and relinquish some of that security.

The tension this suggestion produces comes from the struggle between the emotional self, who would rather stay safe in that familiar comfort zone of what we can control, and, thus, do well, and the rational self, who recognizes the overwhelming evidence validating the new methods (e.g., Angelo, 1993; Weiss, 1992; Whitman, 1988).

A second personal concern about reform, also rarely expressed but often felt, is closely related to the first. The reality is that *many of us do not know how to teach any other way*. Most college science teachers have had no formal education in how to teach. We have learned primarily by examples passed on from our teachers, and those examples have almost exclusively been minor variations on the lecture model. Such a system for training college teachers promotes traditionalism and does not easily admit new developments. Now that the cognitive sciences have added so much to what we know about how people learn, the traditional lecture approach seems stultifying. But where are college teachers to turn to revitalize their classroom techniques? And how are we to gain sufficient experience with new approaches to become as comfortable in front of the podium as behind it?

## So how do we get there from here?

However rationally you may approach change, the decision to adopt active learning strategies carries some emotional implications. The real-

ity need not be as difficult as we expect it to be. If you are lucky, someone in your department may have already started to travel this way, and may share some direction and companionship with you. But if that is not the case, or you just prefer to begin on your own, how do you get started?

First, understand that although some may visualize student-centered approaches as bringing anarchy into the classroom, that is not really the case. The instructor is still in control, but the control is more subtle. The students may have more freedom to explore the content of our courses, and they are definitely on a much longer leash than they are in a lecture setting, but they are still on a leash, and the instructor still guides them through the subject matter. The techniques of classroom management are more democratic than they are in the lecture hall, but they are effective nonetheless. Welty provides some useful examples of management strategies (1989).

Second, and perhaps more importantly, remember that this is *not* an all-or-nothing situation. You are not required to totally abandon what you are doing now. Lecturing can be extremely effective when used in combination with some of these techniques, and it is a simple matter to introduce brief, student-centered teaching methods into a lecture setting. Furthermore, if you ease into them at a comfortable rate, your classroom management skills will grow proportionately as you develop the methodology. Rushing into these methods—as would be true for any new, nontrivial challenge—is a sure road to failure. Be gentle with yourself. Move slowly.

Third, make use of the many resources around you for help, support, and encouragement. As we said before, others have already made the journey and have brought back some excellent directions.

*Peer coaching* is one excellent resource. Although it goes by several names, it is essentially a one-on-one relationship where two teachers help one another expand and deepen their pedagogical expertise. It often focuses on a particular classroom issue. Sometimes one of the teachers is the avowed expert, but usually the relationship is between equals, as its name implies. Some schools have peer coaching programs, where the coaches have been specially trained to do this sort of work; in other cases, the process is more informal.

*Professional development centers* are becoming a more common sight at colleges. These centers also may be called teaching and learning centers, teacher centers, staff development centers, or teaching resource rooms. Their function is to help teachers hone their craft, usually with a "teachers-helping-teachers" approach. The staff at these centers tend to be very responsive to faculty needs and interests. Expressing interest in learning more about student-centered techniques will surely be met with an answer, usually in the form of a workshop.

*Professional societies* are another source of professional development in student-centered teaching strategies. Attending presentations at meetings of the National Science Teachers Association, the Society for College Science Teachers, and/or one of the teaching societies in the science subdisciplines will yield an enormous amount of information about what others are doing in this area. This venue is especially valuable for faculty who find that *they* are the innovators on their campuses and have no one at home to look to for leadership.

*The literature* offers a wide range of advice and direction for the would-be reformer. In the "Two-Year College" column last May, one of us, under the pressure of three simultaneous deadlines, squirmed out of this column's deadline by writing about the things on which he was working (Caprio, 1997a). Those other two publications also described various projects. One, the SCST monograph, contains 14 papers in which colleagues describe the barriers they encountered as they moved toward innovation and how they overcame them (Caprio, 1997b). The other is a handbook for new teachers to help them begin their careers as constructivists in education, as

well as for the more experienced teachers who wish to break (or, perhaps, modify) the old molds (Seibert, et al., 1997).

We recently discovered an excellent text in the proceedings of an NSF-sponsored conference on inquiry approaches to science teaching held at Hampshire College, in June 1996 (McNeal and D'Avanzo, 1997). All of these resources have extensive bibliographies and all of them discuss practical classroom techniques that we do not have the space to describe here.

Finally, remember that active learning approaches to teaching are independent of subject matter and grade level. That may sound strange, but it is true. These methods go to the heart of how people learn. The techniques that work in science classes also work in English classes, and methods used at the elementary level can work in advanced courses, too.

The sad truth is that when it comes to student-centered approaches to teaching, college science teachers are among the last to join the movement. Elementary, middle, and high schools have been in this mode for some time now. Undergraduate English classes we sat in many years ago were already student-centered and were not even considered especially innovative for their time. We must not overlook opportunities to learn from *all* our colleagues.

Help is out there and it is accessible. Ask directions. You *can* get there from here.

### References

Angelo, T.A. 1993. A "teacher's dozen": Fourteen general research-based principles for improving higher learning in our classrooms. *AAHE Bulletin* 45(8): 3–7.

Bonwell, C.C., and J.A. Eison. 1991. Active learning: Creating excitement in the classroom. *ASHE-ERIC Higher Education Report No. 1.* Washington: D.C. The George Washington University, School of Education and Human Development.

Caprio, M.W. 1994. Easing into constructivism. *Journal of College Science Teaching* 23(1).

Caprio, M.W. 1997a. Bits and pieces: A glance at some of SCST's future publications. *The Journal for College Science Teaching* 26(6): 439-440.

Caprio, M.W., ed. 1997b. *The SCST Monograph Series: From Traditional Approaches Toward Innovation*. Greenville, SC: Society for College Science Teachers.

Frederick, Peter J. 1987. Student involvement: Active learning in large classes, teaching large classes well. In *New Directions of Teaching and Learning*, 45-56. San Francisco: Jossey-Bass.

Halyard, R. 1993. Introductory college-level science courses: The SCST position statement. *Journal of College Science Teaching* 23(1): 29-30.

Leonard, William H. 1997. How do college students learn science? In *Effective Teaching and Course Management for University and College Science Teachers*, ed. E. Siebert, M. Caprio, and C. Lyda. Dubuque, IA: Kendall/Hunt Publishing Co.

Lord, T. 1996. A comparison between traditional and constructivist teaching in college biology. *Innovative Higher Education* 21(3).

McNeal, A.P., and C. D'Avanzo, eds. 1997. *Student-Active Science: Models of Innovation in College Science Teaching*. New York, NY: Saunders College Publishing.

Shipman, Harry L. 1997. Not just a lecturer anymore. In *The SCST Monograph Series: From Traditional Approaches Toward Innovation*, ed. M. W. Caprio. Greenville, SC: Society for College Science Teachers.

Siebert, E., M. Caprio, C. Lyda, eds. 1997. *Introductory Science Courses: Teaching and Classroom Management*. Dubuque, IA: Kendall/Hunt.

Weiss, C.A. 1992. But how do we get them to think? *Teaching Excellence* 4(5): 1–2.

Welty, W.M. 1989. Discussion method teaching: A practical guide. *To Improve the Academy* 8:197–216.

Whitman, N.A. 1988. Peer teaching: To teach is to learn twice. *ASHE-ERIC Higher Education Reports* No. 4. Washington, D.C.: Association for the Study of Higher Education.

Yager, R.E. 1991. The constructivist learning model: Towards real reform in science education. *The Science Teacher* 58(6): 52-57.

# An Experimental Project Approach to Biology

*Mastering the Interdisciplinary Skills at the Core of Science*

CHRIS E. PETERSEN

*I* *n our view a serious deficiency of many introductory science courses is that students learn very little, if anything, about how to do science.*
                                             —Lawson et al., 1990

This message has often been the lament of my colleagues at College of DuPage in Illinois, a community college serving over 33,000 students in the outer Chicago metropolitan area. The majority of students fail to understand how science is conducted and how to interpret communications in science.

Our introductory majors sequence in biology (Biology 101, 102, and 103) was developed along the traditional lines of introductory biological science major requirements of a baccalaureate-granting institution. Each course is subdivided into lecture and laboratory components.

The lecture component is self-descriptive, where student involvement is limited to passive listening and the intake of low-level information. The laboratory component is intended to complement lecture with hands-on and visual experiences. Laboratory exercises are mostly a combination of cookbook experiments where students are all but led to conclusions or subjected to "see-and-memorize" experiences.

While the sequence discusses basic terminology and describes biological processes, it is deficient in promoting critical thinking, quantitative analyses, and professional writing. These interdisciplinary skills are integral to how science is conducted, and developing these skills is essential for success in higher coursework as well as on the job. A similar conclusion has been reached in the Netherlands where a new National Curriculum for Secondary Education in Biology was implemented during the 1993/1994 school year to promote these interdisciplinary skills (Jansen et al., 1997).

An interdisciplinary approach based on critical thinking and experimentation involves students intellectually, facilitating academic growth (Bicak and Bicak, 1990; Bisbee and Kaiser, 1997; Deutch, 1994, 1997; Eyster and Tashiro, 1997; Gardiner, 1998; Kirkpatrick and Pittendrigh, 1984; Lawson et al., 1990; Seago, 1992; Slater, 1997). Seago (1992) argues that the traditional teaching style of having students memorize biology "facts" fails to engage students in learning so that they can build their own framework for thinking. Students need to be encouraged to experimentally explore alternatives to hypotheses in order to develop their own thought processes and gain confidence in doing so. Seago suggests communicating their research in the form of a scientific paper.

Writing must have the clarity in style and completeness of description for the reader to comprehend what has been done in an experiment and the conclusion reached on the part of the author. Writing across the curriculum is a practice that has gained popularity across the nation as a means to reverse declines in literacy among high school and college students (Ambron, 1987; Grant and Piirto, 1994; Harris and Schaible, 1997; Slater, 1997; Stewart, 1989; Taylor and Sobota, 1998). Scientific paper writing contributes to this practice.

In the following study, I examined the educational benefits of an experimental project approach to students taking the last course of the introductory sequence, Biology 103. Educational benefits were defined in terms of analytical skills, knowledge of basic statistics, and experience with scientific writing. The study was viewed as a preliminary investigation, but one that involved a critical review of the teaching method.

## Description of Biology 103
Biology 103 provides a partial overview of the Domain Eucarya and discussion of basic concepts in ecology. Laboratory exercises involve reviewing representative organisms and exploring methodology in the experimental testing of simple hypotheses.

Biology 103 is also taught as the last biology course in the two-course honors sequence. Honors Biology 103 requires a research paper, exposing these students more to additional scientific writing. The general description of the research and paper that follows is the same for the two-course honors sequence. The research topic is typically left up to the student, but its design must be very basic because of the scarcity of supporting equipment.

Since most if not all of the students lack statistics training, statistical analyses of experimental findings are limited to eyeballing differences between sample means and performing basic

tests such as t-tests. The honors students submit the paper according to a scientific format presented in the journal *Ecology* found in the college's library. The paper is edited once and the student is then asked to submit a revision.

## The experiment
My approach to Biology 103 involved replacing the ecology and environmental science exercises with a class experiment that required five weeks to conduct and statistically evaluate. Students in single sections of a regular ($R_p$) and honors ($H_p$) Biology 103 performed the class experiment during the spring quarter of 1998. Class sizes for the $R_p$ and $H_p$ sections were 21 and 18 students, respectively. A single section of regular ($R_c$) Biology 103 from the summer quarter of 1997 and a single section of honors ($H_c$) Biology 103 from the spring quarter of 1997 served as controls taught using the traditional approach. Class sizes for the $R_c$ and $H_c$ were 20 and 19 students, respectively.

The objective of the class experiment was to examine the relationships of macro invertebrate community structure in topsoil with the surrounding flora, soil chemistry, and physical factors of a nature preserve on the east side of the college campus. Students were given the objective, a fictitious budget for the research, and an application for the collecting permit. Three students per class were arbitrarily requested to balance the budget. They had to justify the choice of equipment used based on cost and value with respect to the objective of the study. Three other students per class were assigned to fill out the collecting permit application.

During the second week of the quarter, students from the $R_p$ and $H_p$ classes established 24 study sites transecting the nature preserve. Sampling included collecting topsoil and recording plant diversity, soil pH, topsoil temperature, and surface light absorbance. Three students per class were in charge of taking field measurements and recording findings. The remaining class members visually investigated the habitats. The collected

**Table 1.**
E1E2 (Exam 1 + Exam 2 scores) and assessment test mean scores + standard deviation according to treatment and class type. Sample or class sizes are given in parenthesis with E1E2 scores. Symbols: R=regular class section, H=honors class section, c=control treatment, and p=project treatment.

| Treatment | E1E2 | Data interpretation | Basic statistical knowledge | Knowledge scientific paper |
|---|---|---|---|---|
| $R_c$ | 156±25(20) | 3.50±2.04 | 2.60±1.05 | 1.80±1.24 |
| $H_c$ | 165±20(19) | 3.53±2.01 | 2.26±0.87 | 2.26±1.37 |
| $R_p$ | 141±25(21) | 3.81±1.86 | 2.86±1.28 | 2.76±1.30 |
| $H_p$ | 162±21(18) | 5.28±2.04 | 3.00±1.28 | 3.50±0.86 |
| Maximum points possible for parameter | 200 | 10 | 4 | 4 |

soil was used for extracting macroinvertebrates and for measuring moisture and organic content. After retrieving the macroinvertebrates with a Tullgren funnel, a student from each class identified them based on morphotype. The rest of the class double-checked the student's efforts. Students summarized their macroinvertebrate data using correspondence analysis (CA) (Pielou, 1984), tested the first two CA axes for correlation with plant diversity, and took chemical and physical measurements.

I spent 30 minutes discussing what CA is and how inferences can be made from significant correlations between the first two axes of CA and environmental measurements. I then assigned three students per class to review the data, state what could be statistically interpreted from the data, and field remaining questions from the class. As data were gathered, students were asked to enter information into a software program for analysis. The project was rounded off with a scientific paper assignment where students had to draw conclusions from the results.

## The scientific paper

During the third week of the class, students were asked to explain the purpose(s) of each part of a scientific paper and submit their understanding as a graded written assignment. After a 20-minute discussion on how to use our library, students began a search of literature (i.e., texts and science periodicals) relevant to the experiment. Internet sources of information that had not been published in refereed journals and encyclopedias were not acceptable as literature citations.

The first draft of the paper, worth 10 percent of the course grade, was handed in during the seventh week of the quarter. I edited and graded the papers for clarity, literature research, format, and analysis. I then returned the papers to the students to revise. The revised version, due within the week, was worth 5 percent of the course grade. The remainder of the course grade was based on tests, practicals, and assignments. Assignments included jobs given as part of the project.

---

**Table 2.**

Significant comparison of testing parameters according to sections tested, t value, degree of freedom, and probability.

| Comparison | t | degree of freedom | p |
|---|---|---|---|
| Data interpretation honors course sections | 2.55 | 35 | 0.015 |
| Basic statistical knowledge honors course sections | 2.05 | 35 | 0.048 |
| Knowledge of scientific paper regular course sections | 2.42 | 39 | 0.020 |
| Knowledge of scientific paper honors course sections | 3.27 | 35 | 0.002 |

---

## Assessment

Exams 1 and 2 were given during the first five weeks of the quarter. The compiled scores of these tests (annotated by E1E2) were used as indicators of the academic potential of students from all course sections and treatments. An assessment test (available from the author upon request) given during the tenth week of the quarter was used to gauge analytical skills, basic statistics knowledge, and understanding about writing a scientific paper.

Two test questions were used to assess analytical skills. The first question was concerned with an experiment that lacked a control and replication; hence, experimental conclusions could not be made. The second question focused on an experiment that was better constructed, but which required students to understand the value of increased replication for testing treatment effects. Basic knowledge of statistics and scientific writing were assessed using a pair of questions each. As scientific writing was an assignment in both treatments, the a priori prediction was that $H_c$ students would perform equally well on knowledge of scientific paper writing as the $H_p$ group.

## Findings and conclusion

E1E2 and assessment scores are summarized in Table 1 according to section and treatment. Nonsignificant differences in mean E1E2 scores of like sections between treatments did not indicate higher academic skills or abilities among students within the project treatment. Table 2 lists statistical comparisons in assessment scores that were significant ($p < 0.05$) between treatments. Although $R_p$ mean scores were all greater than $R_c$ scores, only the score measuring knowledge of the scientific paper was significantly higher. In contrast, $H_p$ students performed better than $H_c$ students on each of the three components of the assessment test.

The significant differences in assessment testing between $H_p$ and $H_c$ surprised me since the honors students from both treatments had written scientific papers in the previous course, honors Biology 102. However, the explanation might be the ease of the Biology 102 and $H_c$ projects where analysis involved a single comparison. I have come to question the value of such a straightforward exercise because students seem to have no trouble writing a paper based on the assignment, especially if I help with the data analysis. However, when questioned about their work, few have shown a good grasp of the conclusions to be drawn.

In the current project approach, the subject material was unfamiliar to the students and the complexity of the experiment was far greater than a single comparison. Students had to do extensive research and examine how to derive meaning from the relatively large data set. They were actively engaged through classroom discussions and were more involved in understanding the project, interpreting data, and writing the scientific paper. Even the revised draft of the scientific paper was demanding because most students had to rethink aspects of their papers, such as the logic of their explanation or the phrasing of their logic. The greater attention that students had to give to the project may explain the higher scoring by $H_p$ students on the assessment test.

I am not sure how students appreciated the project, although cooperative-learning experiences like mine have been well received by students in science courses (Howard and Boone, 1997; Kerns, 1996). Most of my students seemed to enjoy the fieldwork but the statistical analyses confounded them. I needed time to explain the statistical analyses beyond the time available in the classroom. Many students also confused the results with conclusions. These students had to be told that they must gain an understanding of the significance of their findings with respect to the experimental objective. Students frequently struggle with the thought processes in problem-based learning exercises (Jacobs and Moore, 1998; Shelton and Smith, 1998).

Some criticism of the project approach has been directed at the extensive time instructors need to put into class preparation, helping students, and editing papers (Grant and Piirto, 1994; Magnusun-Martinson, 1996). I found that organization was key to keeping students on track. I spent about eight extra hours a week offering students individual help. Most of my time was spent editing and reading drafts of the scientific papers.

Overall, I devoted about 60 hours editing first and second drafts.

My findings indicate that the project approach helps to develop interdisciplinary skills used in science. Based on assessment testing, students exposed to the project approach performed higher than those not exposed to data interpretation, basic statistics, and the structure of a scientific paper. I have to caution, however, that the findings were limited to a small sample size, although my results are bolstered by the literature. Expanded use of the project approach coupled with continued assessment will more rigorously test its value to the education of undergraduate students.

The project approach is highly applicable to undergraduate education because it directly engages the students in the process of science. Students investigate and experiment to develop their own interpretations of biological processes while enhancing their critical thinking and learning interdisciplinary skills. Based on my experience, I have become a firm believer in the value of the project approach to undergraduate science instruction.

### Acknowledgment

*The author would like to thank B. Petersen for the valuable comments during the preparation of the manuscript.*

### Note

*This project was supported by the Innovation Incubator Program at College of DuPage, IL.*

### References

Ambron, J. 1987. Writing to improve learning in biology. *Journal of College Science Teaching* 17:263-266.

Bicak, C. J., and L. J. Bicak. 1990. Connections across the disciplines. *Journal of College Science Teaching* 20:336-339,346.

Bisbee, G. D., and C.A. Kaiser. 1997. Milkweed seed dispersal: A means for integrating biology and physics. *The American Biology Teacher* 59:426-427.

Deutch, C. E. 1994. Restructuring a general microbiology laboratory into an investigative experience. *The American Biology Teacher* 56:294-296.

Deutch, C. E. 1997. Using data analysis problems in a large general microbiology course. *The American Biology Teacher* 59:396-402.

Eyster, L. S., and J. S. Tashiro 1997. Using manipulatives to teach quantitative concepts in ecology. *The American Biology Teacher* 59:360-364.

Gardiner, L. F. 1998. Why we must change: The research evidence. *Thought & Action, The NEA Higher Education Journal* 14:71-80.

Grant, M. C., and J. Piirto. 1994. Darwin, dogs, and DNA: Freshman writing about biology. *Journal of Science Education and Technology* 3:259-262.

Harris, D. E., and R. Schaible. 1997. Writing across the curriculum can work. *Thought & Action, The NEA Higher Education Journal* 13:31-40.

Howard, R. E., and W. J. Boone. 1997. What influences students to enjoy introductory science laboratories? *Journal of College Science Teaching* 27:383-387.

Jacobs, D., and R. Moore. 1998. Concept-driven teaching and assessment in invertebrate zoology. *Journal of Biological Education* 32:191-199.

Jansen B. J., M. J. Dijkstra, and A. Bloem. 1997. A new curriculum for ethology and student skills in the Netherlands. *The American Biology Teacher* 59:404-410.

Kerns, T. 1996. Should we use cooperative learning in college chemistry? Examining the history of a common pedagogical technique. *Journal of College Science Teaching* 26:435-438.

Kirkpatrick, L. D., and A. S. Pittendrigh.1984. A writing Teacher in the physics classroom. *The Physics Teacher* 22:151-164.

Lawson, A. E., S. W. Rissing, and S. H. Faeth. 1990. An inquiry approach to nonmajors biology. *Journal of College Science Teaching* 20:340-346.

Magnusun-Martinson, S. 1996. A wacky proposal for writing across the curriculum. *Thought & Action, The NEA Higher Education Journal* 12:99-101.

Pielou, E. C. 1984. *The Interpretation of Ecological Data.* New York: John Wiley & Sons.

Seago, J. L. 1992. The role of research in undergraduate instruction. *The American Biology Teacher* 54:401-405.

Shelton, J. B., and R. F. Smith. 1998. Problem-based learning in analytical science undergraduate teaching. *Research in Science and Technological Education* 16:19-29.

Slater, T. F. 1997. The effectiveness of portfolio assessments in science. *Journal of College Science Teaching* 27:315-318.

Stewart, B. 1989. Merging scientific writing with the investigative laboratory. *Journal of College Science Teaching* 19:94-95.

Taylor, K. L., and S. J. Sobota. 1998. Writing in biology. *The American Biology Teacher* 60:350-353.

# The Antimicrobial Properties of Red Algae

*The Fight of Your Life:*
*Battling Bacteria*

CHRISTINE L. CASE AND MICHAEL WARNER

**A** research project provides an ideal opportunity for students to practice scientific techniques and develop their problem-solving skills. Most students majoring in the biological sciences never encounter research opportunities, yet most students want this experience (Carter et al., 1990).

According to the National Research Council and National Science Foundation, an undergraduate science education should prepare students to become both science-literate citizens and competent science professionals (Fort, 1995). To make an informed decision to pursue a career in science, students must experience the doing of science, not just the learning of facts. In putting into practice what they learn in theory, students must have training in making deductions and observations, using pro-

cess skills, and thinking critically (Boud et al., 1980). While these skills are essential to a career in science (Price and Driscoll, 1997), too few lab exercises sufficiently challenge the students' ability to reason at higher levels (Sundberg, 1991).

In undergraduate research programs, however, students can complete original research projects while working closely with trained experts: the professors themselves (Russo, 1997). Barna and Winstead (1993) believe instructors benefit from the collaborative endeavor by acting as role models for students and, a more practical consideration, maintaining their lab skills, in the end becoming better-trained scientists.

At Skyline College in San Bruno, CA, sophomores majoring in biological sciences conduct their own research projects, reviewing literature and designing and conducting laboratory experimentation, under the guidance of a faculty member.

> *Undergraduate research gives students the chance to put biological principles into practice and instructors the chance to supervise research close to their interests and expertise. This article describes a research project in which a professor and student collaborated in the screening of macroscopic algae for antimicrobial properties.*

The research program is designed to (1) actively engage students in their learning, (2) foster independent thinking, and (3) encourage self-directed study. A few students have presented their research project findings at local scientific meetings. Here, we describe one of the research projects completed in the course.

## Background

With Fleming's discovery of penicillin in the late 1920s, the golden age of antibiotics began. Antibiotics have been considered miracle drugs because of their ability to treat bacterial infections without harming healthy human cells. During the last half-century, however, bacteria have developed resistance to many antibiotics. There are some strains of bacteria, including *Pseudomonas aeruginosa*, *Enterococcus faecalis*, and *Mycobacterium tuberculosis*, for which there are no effective antibiotics.

Ironically, antibiotics themselves promote resistance. Through natural selection, the most fit bacteria, that is, the antibiotic-resistance ones, will survive and pass on resistance traits. Levy (1998) states that antibiotics are misprescribed more than 50 percent of the time, resulting in a grave overreliance on antibiotics. The repercussions of this are evidenced by the number of people who have died in recent years from systemic bacterial infections that did not respond to antibiotics. The solution to this quandary is multidimensional, requiring more responsible use of antibiotics and the development of novel antibiotic compounds.

Since 1942, when Pratt (Lustigman, 1988) discovered the antibacterial activity of chlorellin from the green algae, *Chlorella*, a number of researchers have looked to the sea for antimi-crobics. Algae from the coastal waters of Great Britain, France, Italy, Brazil, South Africa, India, United States, Saudi Arabia, the Philippines, and Australia, among others, have been sampled for antibacterial properties (Konig et al., 1994; Konig and Wright, 1997; Mahasneh, 1995; Vlachos, 1996).

In this study, we (professor and student) worked together to screen macroscopic algae for antimicrobial properties against selected gram-positive and gram-negative bacteria. We used the agar-diffusion method, a well-established technique for testing natural sources for antimicrobial properties, to screen algal pieces and algal extracts (Crueger and Crueger, 1989; Krieg and Gerhardt, 1994).

## Materials and methods

We collected the algae listed in Table 1 from several sites in the Monterey Bay National Marine Sanctuary and the Gulf of the Farralones National Marine Sanctuary. The algae were removed from the intertidal zone and frozen at -5°C within 12 hours of collection. We obtained *Staphylococcus aureus*, *Escherichia coli*, and *Pseudomonas aeruginosa* bacteria from the Skyline College Culture Collection.

Nutrient agar plates were inoculated with 100 µL of a 24-hour bacterial culture. Within 24 hours of collection, we rinsed the algal samples with sterile water and placed one-cm pieces on the inoculated plates for an agar diffusion assay. The plates were then incubated for 24 hours and checked for zones of inhibition. We ran controls with 10 µg disks of ampicillin against the gram-positive bacteria and 30 µg disks of tetracycline against the gram-negative bacteria. If we observed an initial zone of inhibition then we incubated the plates for an additional 24 hours to evaluate whether resistant organisms would grow.

Finally, we rinsed samples of *Osmundea spectabilis* (approximately 18–20 cm in size with blades that are flat and pinnate) with sterile water and mechanically ground the samples with a mortar and pestle in each of the following solvents: methanol, ethanol, and methyl chloride.

## Results and discussion

Most algae demonstrated minimal or no zone of inhibition in the agar diffusion assay (Table 1). A few algae, however, especially *O. spectabilis*, did cause a zone of inhibition. Of particular note was the fact that, after 24 hours, *P. aeruginosa* began to grow in the tetracycline zone of inhibition but not in the *O. spectabilis* zone of inhibition.

We used agar-diffusion on nutrient agar plates with *P. aeruginosa* to test extracts of *O. spectabilis*, looking for an appropriate solvent for the antimicrobial metabolite(s). We then tested extracts of *O. spectabilis* to find a solvent for extracting the active compound. We observed no zones of inhibition from the methanol and ethanol extracts of *O. spectabilis*, although the methyl chloride extract produced a 1.8-cm zone of inhibition against *P. aeruginosa*. Methyl chloride alone did not inhibit growth of *P. aeruginosa*.

After performing this study, we discovered that methyl chloride extracts containing the active ingredients in the red alga, *O. spectabilis*, have the potential to treat bacterial infections, especially against *P. aeruginosa*. Antibacterial properties have been observed in *Osmundea* spp., which are found in warmer waters (Konig et al.,1994, Konig and Wright, 1997); *O. spectabilis*, however, is found in cold water throughout the intertidal zones along the California coast. At present, we are characterizing the active metabolites in *O. spectabilis*.

This type of research, besides being topical and relevant, offers students experience in the lab. Russo (1997) states that students need to repeat lab techniques to master them as well as verify results and eliminate errors. Research projects give students just this experience.

**Table 1.**
Bacterial inhibition of selected bacteria by algal pieces in an agar diffusion assay.

+ with no diameter £ 2mm zone of inhibition; ND = not done

| | **Presence of zone of inhibition against** | | |
|---|---|---|---|
| **Algae** | **S. aureus** | **E. coli** | **P. aeruginosa** |
| *Osmundea spectabilis* | + (6 mm diameter zone of inhibition) | + (8 mm diameter zone of inhibition) | + (14 mm diameter zone of inhibition) |
| *Callithamnion pikeanum* | - | - | - |
| *Mazzaella flaccida* | - | - | - |
| *Mastocarpus pappillata* | - | - | - |
| *Neorhodomela larix* | + | + | + |
| *Odonthalia floccosa* | + | + | + |
| *Mazzaella heterocarpa* | - | - | - |
| *Porphyra perforata* | + | - | - |
| *Pelvetiopsis limitata* | - | - | - |
| *Fucus gardneri* | + | - | - |
| Tetracycline, 30 µg | ND | + (26 mm diameter zone of inhibition) | + (9.5 mm diameter zone of inhibition) |
| Ampicillin, 10 µg | + (18 mm diameter zone of inhibition) | ND | ND |

> **Table 2.**
> **Selected original research conducted by Skyline College students and presented at scientific meetings, 1995–1998.**
>
> - Development of Metal Tolerance in Bacteria in Drinking Water Distribution Systems.
> - Novel Antimicrobial Agents Against *Staphylococcus aureus*.
> - Antimicrobial Properties of Juglone, a Walnut Metabolite.
> - The Prevalence of Antibiotic Resistance in Deep Subsurface Bacteria.
> - Development of Resistance in *Enterococcus faecalis* Exposed to Ampicillin or Garlic.
> - A Biological Method to Test the Effectiveness of Sunscreens.
> - Evaluation of Juglone to Prevent Post–Harvest Decay.
> - Identification of Deep Subsurface Bacteria.

## Acknowledgments

*The authors would like to thank Ellen Gartside and Natalie Consantino for assisting with the collection and identification of the algae, Pat Carter for supplying and preparing materials, and Don Biederman and Janice Montagne for critically reading the manuscript.*

## References

Barna, J. and J. Winstead. 1993. Harvey Mudd College: Technology integration offers unique opportunities for undergraduates. *T.H.E. Journal* 21:105-108.

Boud, D. J., J. Dunn, T. Kennedy, and R. Thorley. 1980. The aims of science laboratory courses: a survey of students, graduates and practising scientists. *European Journal of Science Education* 2:415-428.

Carter, J.L., F. Heppner, R. H. Saigo, G. Twitty, and D. Walker. 1990. The state of the biology major. *BioScience* 40:678-682.

Crueger, W. and A. Crueger. 1989. *Biotechnology.* 2nd ed. Sunderland MA: Sinauer.

Fort, D. 1995. Top federal science agencies join other reformers to focus on the vital undergraduate years. *Journal of College Science Teaching* 24:26-31

Konig, G. M. and A.D. Wright. 1997. *Laurencia rigida*: chemical investigations of its antifouling dichloromethane extract. *Journal of Natural Products* 60:967–970.

Konig, G. M., A. D. Wright, O. Sticher, C. K. Angerhofer, and J. M. Pezzuto.1994. Biological activities of selected marine natural products. *Planta Medica* 60:532–538.

Krieg, N. and P. Gerhardt. 1994. Solid, Liquid/Solid, and Semisolid Culture, pp. 216-223. In *Methods for General and Molecular Microbiology,* ed. P. Gerhardt. Washington, D.C.: American Society for Microbiology.

Levy, S. B. 1998. The challenge of antibiotic resistance. *Scientific American* 278: 46–53.

Lustigman, B. 1988. Comparison of antibiotic production from four ecotypes of the marine alga, *Dunaliella. Bulletin of Environmental Contamination and Toxicology* 40:18–22.

Mahasneh, I., M. Jamal, M. Kashashneh, and M. Zibdeh. 1995. Antibiotic activity of marine algae against multi-antibiotic resistant bacteria. *Microbios* 83: 23–26.

Price, E. A., and M. P. Driscoll. 1997. An inquiry into the spontaneous transfer of problem-solving skill. *Contemporary Educational Psycholology* 22:472-494.

Russo, E. 1997. Undergraduate summer research provides taste of laboratory life. *The Scientist* 11:1, 9.

Sundberg, M. D. 1991. Are we reinventing the wheel? *BioScience* 41:779-783.

Vlachos, V., A. T. Critchley, and A. von Holy. 1996. Establishment of a protocol for testing antimicrobial activity in southern African macroalgae. *Microbios* 88: 115–123.

# Inquiry in the Community College Biology Lab

*A Research Report and a*
*Model for Making It Happen*

EDDIE LUNSFORD

Over the years, calls for reforming the way science is taught have intensified. Central to the reform movement is the assertion that learning science should be an active process (NSTA, 1996). Science instruction should be authentic (it should match what real scientists do [Roth, 1995]). Enger and Yager (1998) remind us that good science instruction is multidimensional. It should not only include the facts and content of science (the concept domain) but also should allow students to understand how science actually works (the nature of science domain).

Students must be allowed to design experiments and test their own hypotheses. They must measure, manipulate variables, and apply knowledge in new situations. These are facets of the process, application, attitude, and creativity domains of science.

*A qualitative analysis of students' reactions and outcomes to a long-term inquiry experience in a freshman biology course shows positive results. Students posed research questions and designed experiments. The analysis shows that students reacted favorably and understood the scientific method, the nature of science, and basic biology content.*

Most science instruction tends to be focused on the facts, content, and memorization of the concept domain. Little attention is given to the other five domains of science (Foster, 1998). Community college science instruction tends to be modeled on the lecture-based style of teaching so common at the university level. This type of instruction allows little opportunity for students to be actively engaged in authentic science. It does little to foster understanding or intellectual independence (AAAS, 1990; Roth, 1995). The laboratory experiences we offer students are probably better than nothing. However, they often involve little more challenge than following the step-by-step process of mixing a written recipe. Some writers call such activities "cookbook labs" (Roth, 1995; NSTA, 1996).

Most reform-minded science educators are quick to mention the need to bring "inquiry" into science classrooms at all levels of education.

Much has been written about scientific inquiry as an instructional practice. Inquiry is appealing because it mirrors the work done by scientists. It is authentic and relates to science in an intimate way. Inquiry focuses on posing and answering scientific questions. It actively engages students in gathering evidence (AAAS, 1990). Students make observations, seek out the work of other scientists, use laboratory equipment, think critically, plan, predict, and explain (Keefer, 1998; National Research Council, 1996).

Teachers and researchers have offered terminology to describe variations on the basic process of inquiry as an instructional technique. The terms "collaborative inquiry" or "community inquiry" are used to stress that groups of students may work together (NSTA, 1996). "Purposeful inquiry" is used when the teacher provides students with a research question or when a specific skill or objective is being focused on in the inquiry (Foster, 1998). The term "guided inquiry" is a commonly used synonym for this form. "Open inquiry" or "free inquiry" are labels often applied to the more pure, open-ended inquiry activities.

## Studying reform

The study involved 12 students in a freshman general biology course at a community college in western North Carolina. Census data are presented for purposes of general interest. Students ranged from 17 to 39 years of age, with the mean age being 27.5. Five students were female and 7 were male. They were enrolled in the school's College Transfer Program and listed majors as diverse as business, sports management, and education. Only 1 student reported having taken another college science course, a one-semester general chemistry class.

Four questions are central to this research project:

- How will students react to conducting a long-term inquiry activity?
- Will they be able to design and carry out a collaborative inquiry project?

- Will participation help students better understand the scientific method (SM) and nature of science (NOS)?
- Will participation help students learn biology content other than SM and NOS?

The instructor had specific aspects of NOS in mind before beginning this research. He wanted students to understand that (1) science is a creative endeavor driven by both imagination and logic, (2) scientific knowledge is not authoritarian but is tentative and subject to change, (3) science often represents a sociocultural activity, and (4) science is not totally objective (Schwartz, Lederman, and Crawford, 2000; AAAS, 1990).

Data were collected by three methods. The course instructor monitored students' reactions and work. Students completed an anonymous written survey near the end of the study and were required to write a formal lab report summarizing their group's inquiry activity. The instructor used this lab report to assign grades based on an assessment of students' work and understanding. These papers were analyzed with the research questions of this study in mind.

## Model research

Students had already received some instruction on course objectives pertinent to the inquiry activity. They had studied some aspects of SM and NOS, the differences between scientific research and review papers, and how to recognize the various parts of scientific research papers. The decision regarding how much instruction to give students before an inquiry depends on the type of inquiry used and the discretion of the teacher.

Students began the six-week inquiry by brainstorming. They listed living organisms they were interested in working with that were inexpensive, small, and easy to maintain. About 40 organisms were suggested. Each student was then invited to share any strong feelings concerning any organisms on the list. The list was reduced to five organisms. Students unanimously voted to study crickets. Two students knew sources for *Achetus domesticus,* a European cricket widely cultivated and sold in local bait shops. They suggested using this organism for the inquiry, and the other students agreed. The instructor and some students made arrangements to obtain crickets and to provide a habitat for them in the lab using 40-liter aquariums. Additional crickets were placed in the tanks as necessary. Working in small lab groups, students created a list of potential "researchable questions" on which they could base their inquiry.

Throughout the inquiry, the instructor acted as a facilitator. He observed each lab group, answered a few questions, and made pertinent suggestions. Otherwise, he played a minimal role. Students were told how to differentiate between male and female crickets. The teacher made common lab materials available (rulers, lamps, and thermometers) and helped procure specific materials students requested (graph paper, compass, and beakers).

## Research results

Students began work on their inquiry projects quickly. The instructor assumed that students would need time to hone their group's research question, better acquaint themselves with the research organism, and get past uncertainties he had expected them to display. He was surprised when all groups brought equipment to the first lab period of the inquiry and began working instantly. All groups used an aquarium as the core of their experimental apparatus.

Throughout the study, many students displayed great curiosity about the cricket *A. domesticus*. Students found the scientific name of the organisms, information about its native habitat, other genera and species of crickets, diet, reproductive behavior, and other aspects of the organism. Students found that there is a sizeable industry built around cultivating *A. domesticus* as fishing bait.

By the second week of the inquiry activity, students wanted to conduct shorter but more fre-

quent experimental trials. The instructor accommodated this request by devoting a portion of both weekly class meetings to the inquiry. Figure 1, next page, lists total numbers of student behaviors and responses relating to the research questions of this study.

Students reacted favorably regarding the inquiry experience. All students made at least one positive comment. Only one negative comment was recorded. The following are examples of students' written comments:

- I would recommend this type of approach to understanding not only the scientific method but to science in general.
- I enjoyed the cricket lab, although I did think a lot of it was kind of useless. Crickets die quickly, they stink, and are annoying.
- I am disappointed to stop this laboratory. The fact that you attempt to gather information on a subject not fully understood by science is thrilling.
- I liked doing the inquiry because it was different from other labs.

All students demonstrated that they learned biology content during the inquiry. Many technical terms, scientific names, and morphological descriptions filled their lab reports. Because students incorporated the content into their lab reports in appropriate, sensible ways, it is clear that most students understood this array of information. Some content was learned directly from observations of the organism. In other cases, students became curious about a specific thing they had observed and used reference materials to help answer questions or asked the teacher for answers.

The following are selected examples of biology content extracted from students' lab reports and survey responses:

- I learned about the general anatomy of insects.
- I learned about the use of pheromones for communication and breeding.

## Figure 1.

Tally of behavior episodes relating to research question or instructor goal.

| Student response to a research question or instructional goal | Teacher observations | Responses from anonymous student surveys | Response from student laboratory reports | Total |
|---|---|---|---|---|
| Displays explicit positive response to inquiry experience | 15 | 5 | 1 | 21 |
| Displays explicit negative response to inquiry experience | 0 | 1 | 0 | 1 |
| Understands that science is creative and involves imagination and logic | 7 | 9 | 19 | 35 |
| Understands that scientific knowledge is tentative and subject to change | 5 | 10 | 12 | 27 |
| Understands that science is a social-cultural activity | 3 | 6 | 16 | 25 |
| Understands that science is not totally objective | 4 | 6 | 14 | 24 |
| Understands the scientific method | 10 | 14 | 37 | 61 |
| Is exposed to biology content other than SM and NOS | 3 | 8 | 28 | 39 |

- *A. domesticus* is polyphagous, meaning it will eat most any organic substance.
- I learned about chemoreceptors, the different types and where they may be located. The chemoreceptors most pertinent to our research are called sensilla.
- I found out about the efforts of the pest control industry to develop powerful pheromone-based baits and traps, which would mean less use of dangerous pesticides.
- I learned about the cricket life cycle, reproduction, and courtship.

Results relating to students' understandings of SM and NOS were mixed. Generally, students did well. Each student displayed behaviors or made statements suggesting some degree of mastery. Some students showed a less-than-stellar understanding of the basics. Two things proved difficult for some students. The first was interpreting data to reach a conclusion. The second was the need to run multiple experimental trials to replicate results and reach valid conclusions. A few students failed to provide adequate detail in their lab reports on measurements, methodology, and operational definitions. Many students liberally and inappropriately used words such as "proved" and "disproved."

Other written evidence was more encouraging. Most students said that their tests were inconclusive. Some specifically stated the need for additional experimental trials. Others suggested specific ways in which their procedure could be modified to produce more reliable results, or they raised additional research questions. The teacher witnessed numerous events indicating that students had made realizations about SM and NOS. Many students were pleased to discover published references detailing research similar to theirs. One lab group found research that mirrored its own. This group tried to determine if *A. domesticus* would detect and avoid the odor of a predator, the wolf spider, *Lycosa aspersa*. They found scientific literature in which the research question was essentially reversed. (Would *L. aspersa* detect and respond to the odor of a cricket species it commonly preyed upon?)

In their lab reports, students noted that they would have liked to have been able to measure and collect predator odors in a more sophisticated fashion. One member of this group even suggested that he would like to try the group's final experimental method with a species of predator that *A. domesticus* would encounter in its native habitat.

A second group had an interesting set of experiences that helped them better understand SM and NOS. Students divided an aquarium into two large lateral compartments and a smaller middle compartment. They hooked a humidifier to one of the larger compartments and introduced their crickets into the smaller compartment. At the end of their first experimental trial, they found that all of the crickets had congregated in the less humid side of the tank. The students announced, "We're through! We are convinced."

The instructor told the group that their results looked promising. He asked the group if any other variable could have produced the results. One student said that the crickets might have been trying to avoid the noise of the humidifier. They ran a second trial and got a very different set of results. Next, they modified their procedure and began to humidify the aquarium before they introduced the crickets. On their own, they abandoned their original hypothesis and began to study the possibility of directional influences on the crickets' movements.

A second discussion among the group members and teacher occurred. One student suggested that they were observing only random activity of the crickets. A second student suggested that some sort of visual or chemical signal could be causing most of the crickets to consistently cluster together within the tank.

The inquiry aspect is more than just the actual testing of the hypothesis. It includes the research of fundamental information needed to design, assemble, and perform the test. Ideas and information sometimes come from strange but reliable sources. More questions are created in the lab than are answered.

## Summary and Discussion

This article presents a useful and adaptable model by which college science instructors can incorporate inquiry into their classrooms. The model is appealing for several reasons. It allows students to generate and research their own scientific questions, work on a long-term project, and practice working as a team. It is of an open-ended nature and consistent with democratic classroom practices.

Students who participated in this research study are representative of the typical community college population. They have widely ranging backgrounds, ages, and interests. It is therefore reasonable to suggest that other students could enjoy similar experiences. There is overwhelming evidence that students reacted positively to this experience with inquiry, learned biology content, and walked away with solid understandings of what science is about and how scientists work.

The few students who had trouble drawing sound conclusions and who struggled with the idea of experimental replication do not complicate the findings of this research. The interpretation of scientific data is often, after all, a sophisticated cognitive skill. Also, some of these students may have held deeply ingrained preconceptions about science. Additional exposure to inquiry activities would probably help those students to better master additional concepts and sharpen their skills.

Clearly, there is a need for community college science teachers to include inquiry in their teaching or to broaden their current use of it. Other studies appearing in *JCST* support this view (Grant and Vatnick, 1998; Silvius and Stutzman, 1998). Teachers should share their experiences and ideas with others. A study comparing attitudes and knowledge about the nature and methods of science between students taught by inquiry and those taught with more traditional lecture-dominated methods is clearly needed. This teacher-researcher hypothesizes that such a study would add to the already-convincing evidence that tells us that allowing community college students to experience science is preferable to just telling them about it.

### References

American Association for the Advancement of Science (AAAS). 1990. *Science for All Americans.* New York: Oxford University Press.

Enger, S.K., and R.E. Yager, eds. 1998. *The Iowa Assessment Handbook.* Iowa City: University of Iowa.

Foster, S. 1998. New perspective—new practice: Curriculum as web of inquiry. *Principled Practice in Mathematics and Science Education* 2(1): 1–10.

Grant, B.W., and I. Vatnick. 1998. A multi-week inquiry for an undergraduate introductory biology laboratory. *Journal of College Science Teaching* 28(2):109.

Keefer, R. 1998. Criteria for designing inquiry activities that are effective for teaching and learning science concepts. *Journal of College Science Teaching* 28(3):159.

National Research Council. 1996. *National Science Education Standards.* Washington, D.C.: National Academy Press.

National Science Teachers Association (NSTA). 1996. *NSTA Pathways to the Science Standards.* Arlington, Va.: NSTA.

Roth, W.M. 1995. *Authentic School Science: Knowing and Learning in Open Inquiry Science Laboratories.* Dordrecht, Netherlands: Kluwer Academic Publishers.

Schwartz, R.S., N.G. Lederman, and B. Crawford. 2000. "Making connections between the nature of science and scientific inquiry: A science research internship for preservice teachers." Paper presented at the annual meeting of the Association for the Education of Teachers in Science, Akron, Ohio.

Silvius, J.E., and B.C. Stutzman. 1998. A botany laboratory inquiry experience. *Journal of College Science Teaching* 28(3):193.

# A Two-Sided Mirror of Science Education

*Reflecting on the Distant*
*World of Science to See Close*
*Connections to Everyday Life*

JAMES E. HEATH, JR.

How can we discover what students are thinking about science, their connection to science, and the interaction between science and society? Sometimes students themselves cannot articulate the answers to these questions. So how can we as science educators help students find the answers for themselves?

The technique of critical reflection can be a valuable tool to assist in this endeavor. Moreover, the "mirror" of critical reflection works both ways: students can use it to connect science more to their everyday lives, and instructors can use techniques of critical reflection to inform and improve their teaching practices.

Critical reflection is a process similar to critical thinking, but with a different focus. The skill of critical

thinking generally involves uncovering the underlying assumptions and hidden agendas found in external sources of information, such as media presentations, political messages, and academic literature (Brookfield, 1993). The focus of critical thinking is on giving learners the opportunity to view such sources with healthy skepticism.

The skill of critical reflection is different in an important way. Critical reflection involves analyzing one's own underlying assumptions, an internal source of information. Mezirow and Associates (1990) define critical reflection as "Assessment of the validity of the presuppositions of one's meaning perspectives..." (p. xvi). This makes critical reflection a much more difficult and potentially disturbing task than critical thinking (Brookfield, 1994).

Despite its difficulty and potential pitfalls,

*This paper describes students using critical reflection, the process of thinking about one's opinions and biases, to assume the role of the director of the National Science Foundation and rank five hypothetical government-funded science projects according to funding priority. This exercise, which helps sharpen writing and persuasion skills, motivates students to think about their role as citizens in a technological society.*

the process of critical reflection has been very important to me as a college science instructor. I encourage it in my students, to bring the often distant and esoteric world of science in closer contact with their own world. I also use it to shape (and, I hope, improve) my teaching practices.

In this paper, I present one of the activities I use to encourage critical reflection in my community college students.

## A critical reflection exercise for students

In an effort to make science classes more relevant to students' everyday lives, science instruction should ask students to ponder the role of science in modern society. This need is especially great in college science classes, as college students are typically becoming enmeshed in the political and economic realities of life and need to see science as more than just a dry set of facts divorced from the "real world."

Furthermore, these times demand a voting public well versed in science-society issues since publicly funded research has come under hard budgetary scrutiny by the federal government. It behooves us as scientists and science educators to motivate these future voters (and funding grantors!) to think about the importance of scientific enterprises to society.

When teaching my elementary astronomy class for nonscience majors at Austin Community College, I use a variation on Stephen Brookfield's "Crisis Decision Simulation" (Brookfield, 1987, Chapter 6) to stimulate students to think about the relationship between science and society.

The situation I present to the students was inspired by a test question used by Professor R. Robert Robbins of the University of Texas at Austin. I ask students to assume the role of a National Science Foundation official who must prioritize the funding of five imaginary research proposals. Students then write a three to five page "opinion paper" listing and defending their choices. I provide them with the details of the

paper in a handout similar to **Figure 1**. Students must work on the project individually so that they will focus on their own attitudes and opinions and avoid the possibility of "groupthink." The paper began as an extra-credit activity, but positive student reviews have led me to upgrade it to a permanent part of my grading scheme. It can be worth anywhere from 5 to 10 percent of the final grade, depending on the presence of other projects, such as observation projects.

I have included nonastronomy projects in the list to reflect the diversity of projects that draw on government funds. I want to illustrate to students the competition for government money that astronomy faces from other branches of science. Because of this diversity, this project contributes very little to students' acquisition of course content. However, I feel that the gains students can experience in critical reflection and communication skills more than compensate for the lost opportunities for content acquisition, which is adequately covered in other parts of my class.

I give no specifications on the amount and type of research students must do to support their opinions. I feel that it is important for adult learners to find their own way in this matter. One interesting outcome of this project is a measure of how much research each student feels is necessary to support his or her opinions.

Some students have submitted papers that were purely opinion, and which reflect common misconceptions about issues such as the spread of AIDS, the viability of solar energy technology, and the root causes of world hunger. Other papers have included more research, and students have expressed surprise at how much their research changed their opinions. One student even polled some of her coworkers on how they would prioritize the projects and collected the results.

The issue of assessment is important for such a subjective project. Naturally, I cannot base the grade I assign on how well the writer's opinions conform to my own. Also, since I have given students no strict rules governing research, I cannot use that as part of a fair rubric.

---

**Figure 1.**
Critical Reflection Exercise for Students

**Opinion Paper**

*Much of the information that we have about the universe (indeed, much of our scientific knowledge) has come to us in the past half-century, as the products of government-funded science. The purpose of this paper is to get you to think about what kinds of projects deserve these limited funds.*

*You are in charge of providing researchers with funds from the National Science Foundation (NSF). The NSF has had its funds slashed in recent years by Congress, so money is short. Five projects are on your desk and you must prioritize them with the knowledge that low-priority projects might not get funded. The projects are as follows:*

1. Research and development of revolutionary new solar energy technology for the International Space Station.

2. Research into a treatment for breast cancer involving a rare plant that may soon be extinct.

3. Research into human nutrition to produce a low-cost, high-yield food source in conjunction with a joint U.S.-Russia manned mission to Mars.

4. Research in genetic engineering involving animal immune systems.

5. Construction and launch of a group of radio space telescopes to study distant galaxies and the radiation left over from the Big Bang.

*List the projects in priority order and explain thoroughly your rationale for your choices in a three to five page paper. Pretend that you will have to deal with public opinion and disappointed scientists. You may use outside sources of information or just stick to your own opinions. Remember that there are no wrong or right opinions, only well or poorly defended ones.*

---

I choose, instead, to focus the majority of my assessment on the paper's internal consistency. Note in **Figure 1** that I ask students to explain their rationale for prioritizing the projects. As I read a paper, I make note of how thoroughly the student has articulated his or her criteria for evaluating the projects. Then I check to see how tenaciously the student has clung to these criteria as the paper progresses. I also evaluate clarity of writing style and the student's willingness to acknowledge that other viewpoints exist. A full description of the rubric is given in **Figure 2**.

All of my students have high school diplomas or the equivalent, so they have had training in writing persuasive papers. I have found that

most students can recall this training, just as many recall their high school mathematical training on the homework problems; they merely need a venue to showcase these neglected talents. Over 90 percent of the papers submitted to me in the past five years have been at the four- or five-point level, according to my rubric.

Some instructors may take issue with the fact that I set no boundaries on the amount of research required. This is partly because there are no such boundaries in the real world of fund granting. However, there is a deeper reason: the inclusion of a substantial research component shifts part of the focus to skills of critical thinking, the evaluation of the work of others.

---

**Figure 2.**
Grading Rubric for Opinion Paper

### Grading System for Opinion Paper

*The following will determine your grade:*

- The standards and criteria you use to rank the projects. The standards should be specific and understandable.

- How consistently you use the standards to rank the projects. All five projects need to receive equal consideration, if not equal ranking.

- How clear and understandable your paper is. Avoid the use of jargon. Structure your paper into many paragraphs to make it easy to read. A good way to test it is to ask a classmate to read the paper and point out places where you are unclear—just like scientists do.

*The following will not determine your grade:*

- How well your opinions correlate with mine.

- The number of experts you cite. The amount of research you do is up to YOU.

- The length of the paper. It will be hard to make a very clear argument in less than three pages, however.

- Points will not be specifically taken off for spelling and grammar errors, but these will affect the clarity of your paper, so spell check and proofread!

*I will award up to five points on this paper. Some sample grades:*

0 points:   *No paper turned in.*

1 point:    *Poorly written paper, no clear standards, projects just listed.*

2 points:   *Standards stated, but too broad ("The projects should be good").*

3 points:   *Standards clearly stated, but only weakly connected to ranking.*

4 points:   *Standards clearly stated and connected to ranking, but very little elaboration on why the author feels they are linked.*

5 points:   *Standards are clearly explained and are repeated constantly throughout the ranking process. Author goes into detail about how closely linked the standards are to the ranking. Everything is tied together in a concluding paragraph.*

---

My personal goal for this project is to promote critical reflection, although critical thinking and critical reflection are by no means mutually exclusive. My focus on personal reflection leads me to emphasize developing standards and criteria, consistently applying those standards, and clearly articulating the links between the standards and their rankings. It is certainly valid to require substantial research for this project, but the extra work by both instructor and student would require an expanded rubric and an expanded percentage of the final grade.

I set no boundaries on the format of the paper, giving students an opportunity to exercise creative communication skills. Some students structure their papers as a personal narrative. A common form for the paper is a memo from the "Director of the NSF" to "President Heath."

In many cases, students who have struggled with more quantitative aspects of the class (such as the homework problems) use the paper as a chance to show off their creative talents. Student comments on year-end reviews reflect their appreciation (and apprehension) of this aspect of the paper:

- The NSF [paper] was a good break away from the [homework] and gave us a chance to give our opinions.
- [I] was skeptical of [the NSF paper] because I didn't know if it was correct...Still, a great idea.
- The NSF projects were a nice break to the monotony and detail of the homework/test routine.
- I enjoyed the opinion paper. It was nice to have a little subjective thought in an otherwise fact-based environment.

I am confident that this exercise does have potential to stimulate students to think about the role of science in society, as evinced by many student comments:

- It helped me learn about [how] I prioritize certain issues. It also made me think about the pros of certain issues that I had not thought about (like collaboration with Russia).
- I never enjoy writing papers but I did learn something from it. It made me really think about issues I had never pondered before.
- It forced me to think about science and what science should be responsible for.
- The NSF project was not enjoyable per se but it did give me an opportunity to think about something I otherwise would never have done.
- It linked the practical effects of science with everyday life.

- [The NSF project] really gets you thinking beyond your own little world.
- I found myself backing a cause I really had never thought about before. It...gave me new insight on the importance of pure research.

My goal for this project was to stimulate students to think reflectively about issues of government-funded science, a process that will always be a part of their lives as Americans, directly or indirectly. Judging by the above student reviews, I believe it has been successful.

Appropriately, the critical reflection exercise itself grew out of my own critical reflection as an instructor. I took a long look at the way I taught my astronomy class and noticed that well over 90 percent of my class was focused on acquisition of content. I then reflected on my goals for the class: Was I trying to train future professional astronomers? In most cases, certainly not. So why the overwhelming focus on content? In that moment I decided to concentrate more on developing in my students a positive attitude towards astronomy and its connection to their lives. This critical reflection exercise is part of my effort to accomplish that goal.

Critical reflection is a mirror with two sides. Students can employ it to explore their feelings about science in society and become more informed citizens. Instructors can use it to teach responsively and keep their teaching fresh. The practice of critical reflection is difficult, but enriching.

### Note

*The author especially recommends* The Skillful Teacher (Brookfield, 1990) *as a source of ideas and affirmation for educators at all experience levels. He would also like to thank his colleagues at the University of Texas and Austin Community College for discussions about and reflections on this paper.*

### References

Brookfield, S. 1987. *Developing Critical Thinkers.* San Francisco: Jossey-Bass.

Brookfield, S. 1990. *The Skillful Teacher.* San Francisco: Jossey-Bass.

Brookfield, S. 1993. Breaking the code: Engaging practitioners in critical analysis of adult educational literature. *Studies in the Education of Adults* 23(1): 64-91.

Brookfield, S. 1994. Tales from the dark side: A phenomenology of adult critical reflection. *International Journal of Lifelong Education* 13(3): 203-216.

Mezirow, J., and Associates. 1990. *Fostering Critical Reflection in Adulthood.* San Francisco: Jossey-Bass.

# *LifeLines OnLine—* Curriculum and Teaching Strategies for Adult Learners

## *Integrating Information Technology With Problem-Solving Pedagogies*

ETHEL D. STANLEY AND MARGARET A. WATERMAN

lthough biology courses introduce the requisite life science concepts to undergraduates, the curriculum and pedagogies often fail to prepare students to use what they have "learned" to solve real problems (Stover 1998). As a result, educators and researchers have called for reform in biology education so students can become familiar with the process of science, not just its products (NSF, 1996).

The biology curriculum must provide opportunities for students to access, retrieve, and utilize biological information (Flynn, 1998; Stover, 1998; Ercegovac, 1997; Shotwell, 1996; Eaton, 1993) so they can connect their knowledge to the biological issues they face every day (White, 1988). Inquiry is not just useful in scholarship; asking questions and evaluating information are invaluable skills for daily decision making (Ercegovac and Yamasaki, 1998).

The task of addressing the science literacy issue by way of curricular reform rests largely on the shoulders of two-year college faculty members. According to American Association of Community College projections (1998), the typical undergraduate taking biology within five years will be over the age of 25, working, and enrolled in a two-year college. Therefore, these instructors must locate, adapt, and apply curricular resources and teaching strategies that present biology in meaningful contexts and develop problem-solving skills that are pedagogically consistent with adult learning strategies.

A first step toward developing resources that engage the two-year college student is to make more use of pedagogical strategies that recognize and build upon the prior experience, knowledge, and practical learning strengths of adult students. Adult students tend to immerse themselves in tasks that they see as relevant to situations they are likely to face in their own lives (Knowles, 1984; Ertmer and Dillon, 1998).

Instructors interested in applying appropriate pedagogies for adult learners within the sciences have a choice of science teaching methodologies. For example, collaborative learning is considered a useful addition to the repertoire of teaching methods used in two-year colleges since it "helps prepare students for workplaces that increasingly value self-motivated, self-confident, team-oriented employees" (Cooke, 1994). Another example is the use of narratives of realistic problems or case studies. A recent essay in this journal's case study column (Herreid, 1999) describes the power of such stories in science learning.

Problem-Based Learning (PBL) is a variation of the case study specifically designed for small collaborative groups. Finkle and Torp (1995) define PBL as:

> a curriculum development and instructional system that simultaneously develops both problem-solving strategies and disciplinary knowledge bases and skills by placing students in the active role of problem solvers confronted with an ill-structured problem that mirrors real-world problems.

These "ill-structured problems" or cases have multiple solutions. Resolution of a problem requires students to navigate through a variety of resources, develop supportable problem-solving strategies, and present their conclusions to others. Research by Stepien and Gallagher (1993) shows that PBL enhances self-directed learning and helps students transfer concepts they have learned to new problems.

A second step toward addressing science literacy is to introduce and integrate investigative methodologies into the biology curricula. By linking investigation with PBL case analysis, students will learn biology and scientific practice while exploring realistic and familiar contexts. And if students see these investigative experi-

ences extend their ability to make sense of the science-related problems they face every day, they will be more likely to value and use investigative skills throughout their lives.

## Curricular modules for community college biology

To address these curricular and pedagogical challenges, we are collaborating with two-year college faculty to further develop and field test problem-based, prototype curriculum materials called *LifeLines OnLine*. These curriculum modules begin with realistically complex situations presented as articles in an electronic newspaper accessible on the Internet.

The teaching strategies for *LifeLines OnLine* are a variant of PBL (Barrows and Tamblyn, 1980) called Investigative Case-Based Learning (ICBL) (Waterman, 1998; Waterman and Stanley, 1998). Like many variants of PBL, this is a method of teaching that gives students opportunities to direct their own learning as they explore the science underlying realistic situations. Students work collaboratively to identify issues, frame questions of interest to them, and identify additional information in answer to their questions.

ICBL strategies encourage students to expand their investigation by developing questions and reasonable investigative approaches, gathering data and information testing their hypotheses, and working to persuade others of their findings. Students use a variety of resources to accomplish these tasks including traditional laboratory and field techniques, software simulations and models, data sets, Internet-based tools, and information retrieval methods.

*LifeLines OnLine* materials integrate information technology with investigative case-based learning (ICBL) pedagogies. The initial interface students encounter is an electronic newspaper. In *LifeLines OnLine*, resource materials are packaged for students to use as they investigate the science behind the news. As students read the newspaper, several items will have hyperlinks such as a note on plunging corn futures on the

**Table 1.**
Sample Presentation Strategies by Group.

| Group | Sample Strategies |
| --- | --- |
| Group 1 | Corn crop management—live interview with Mr. Beauchamp, a local corn grower who is also husband of one of the students |
| Group 2 | Role of weather in the spread of blights—research poster featuring screen shots from the Late Blight simulations |
| Group 3 | Spacing impacts on the growth of corn—research poster using lab data |
| Group 4 | Diseases of corn—comparative pathogens poster including images |

stock market page, an editorial cartoon on ineffective corn pesticide use, or a classified ad of a farm for sale. Students click on hyperlinks to get to the resources (e.g., interviews, data, and web sites) related to the corn futures story, the cartoon, and the farm sale.

## Illustrating ICBL and *LifeLines OnLine* modules

Individuals approach learning with cases in very different ways. Likewise, instructors will use *LifeLines OnLine* in a variety of ways. The following classroom scenario illustrates how an instructor uses ICBL with *LifeLines OnLine* materials as an alternative way to teach ecology in an introductory biology course. The six ICBL strategy boxes for instructors (see page 107) show how the materials are used within the broad framework of ICBL strategies. An instructor might choose to use one or more of these after introducing the newspaper "case."

The instructor asked the students to pay special attention to relationships as they worked through the materials. Four groups of six students at a two-year college in the Midwest were working in a corner of the classroom reading a copy of an interview of two scientists about a corn epidemic. The instructor chose the article from the *LifeLines OnLine* web site. One group focused in on the following part of the article:

Derrick Hernandez explained, "What made me decide to study corn diseases was hearing about when my uncle lost his entire corn crop in 1970 due to southern leaf blight. He just couldn't understand why every field in the county was failing." (See ICBL Box 1.)

### Getting started

In order to organize the group's discussion, the instructor provided a Know/Need to Know chart. The students worked together to construct a list of things they already knew and questions they felt they needed to answer.

*What we already know:*
• Corn is an important agricultural crop.
• Corn is planted in the spring and harvested later in the fall and has a long growing season.
• Southern leaf blight kills corn.
• Weather can influence the spread of corn blight.
• Southern leaf blight spreads.

*What we need to know:*
• What can I do to get corn to grow better?
• Where does leaf blight come from?
• What exactly is southern corn leaf blight?
• How is corn blight affected by weather?
• How does it cause crop failure?
• How does blight spread?
(See ICBL Box 2.)

## Next steps, same class period

To answer their questions, the students agreed to spend 30 minutes searching out resources then meet for a few minutes at the end of the period. Among the resources in the room were web addresses from the reporter's notes, a computer with an Internet connection, folders on corn disease and crop management, and several books as well as their own text. (See ICBL Box 3.)

## Continuing in lab

In the lab, the groups examined the effect of plant spacing on the growth of corn. They set up additional pots to test their hypotheses about temperature, water availability, or light variables. One group chose to look at water availability. The students thoroughly watered both pots, but left one pot sitting in a pan of water and the other sitting in a pan of sand.

The second part of lab was devoted to looking at the effect of weather variables on crop yields of potatoes using the software simulation *Lateblight* (Ticknor and Arneson, 1990). Student groups initially compared profits from potato farming during wet, moderate, and dry growing seasons with late blight present. Each group was then asked to explore a variable of their choice such as pesticide applications, protectant sprays, or the use of hybrid potatoes with resistance to blight. (See ICBL Box 4.)

## Next class

In the next lab each of the four groups decided how they were going to present results of their *Lateblight* investigations to the rest of the class. Presentation choices may include designing a group poster that is either research oriented or informational. Round-robin poster sessions, in which each member of the group takes a turn to present the group poster while the nonpresenting members visit other posters, permit students to communicate their work on a personal basis.

Adult learners value face-to-face sessions with "experts" who are approachable. For that reason, interviews are an especially good presentation format. As Table 1 shows, Group 1 has invited a corn grower, who is the spouse of a student in the class, to be interviewed. The group prepared a list of questions beforehand to make the best use of the interview time. (See ICBL Box 5.)

## Exam questions

The instructor used the posters and lab work to evaluate student knowledge of relationships between organisms and environments. Students also submitted a one-page summary of the relationships they have been studying in the corn field ecosystem and related them to larger concepts of ecology they learned in lectures and from their text. To further evaluate the students' processes of investigation and values about science, we used the following exam questions:

Consider the following scenario. *A previously thriving clump of oaks is in trouble. A year ago, moths came in and laid eggs, which produced caterpillars that eat oak leaves. This fall, there are few acorns and many hungry squirrels.*

- Identify three questions you have about this ecosystem.
- Choose one and describe the procedures you might use to answer this question. Be specific. List five types of resources.
- Which one of the above resources would you use first? Why?

*Scientists living in the Biosphere II project (described in class) were surprised that the oxygen level was dropping more rapidly than anticipated. They added more oxygen to the dome, but wanted to look into other solutions. Which one of the following approaches to this problem would you recommend and why?*

- Add more plants to the Biosphere II.
- Analyze samples of soil, water and air for the rate of oxygen consumption and compare to expected rates.
- Put on "moon suits" and oxygen tanks.

**ICBL Strategy Box 1** *Recognize potential issues.* Read the case noting words or phrases that seem to be important to understanding what the case is about. Students are looking for learning issues that they might explore further. If students have a hard copy, they might underline these phrases and jot down ideas and questions about these phrases. If students are working in a group, this approach might be led as a group discussion, with one person keeping a list of issues as they are raised.

**ICBL Strategy Box 2** *Brainstorm for connections.* The specifics of the case should be reviewed to identify potential learning issues or biology problems to investigate. It may be helpful to think about the case as a whole and pinpoint underlying themes. Ask the question: "What is this case about?" Pose specific questions. Another way to generate ideas and connections is to be clear about what is known so far and then see what questions arise. Students might use a chart like the popular "Know/Need to Know" format. See example in text. Define problems further by sharing views and concerns. As learners define problems and frame specific questions to investigate, they must consult with others from their group or their classmates. Talking about ideas and plans with others helps to refine problems and can lead to different perspectives that might shape good research problems. Such discussion and collaboration is a hallmark of the work of scientists.

**ICBL Strategy Box 3** *Obtain additional references/resources.* No matter what type of question learners pose, it is likely they will seek and use additional resources to help them support and formulate a reasonable answer. Resources may include textbooks, other library materials, results of computer simulations, results of lab or field research, articles from professional journals or popular press, data sets, maps, e-mails, web sites or other electronically based resources, pamphlets from organizations, interviews with experts, or information from museum exhibits.

**ICBL Strategy Box 4** *Design and conduct scientific investigations.* Students are encouraged to use available laboratory, field, or computer tools and resources. Students, like scientists, begin by synthesizing pieces of existing information into a new theoretical framework (work that may be accompanied by modeling, as was done by Watson and Crick). They locate datasets, conduct interviews, and gather ideas from their reading and library research as well as from laboratory activities.

**ICBL Strategy Box 5** *Produce materials that support understanding of the conclusions.* When students are ready to present their own conclusions, ask them to identify ways for others to view and review their work. Traditionally, we ask for term papers or lab reports, but the possibilities for other supporting materials are vast, for example, posters, poetry, plays, videos, booklets, pamphlets, consulting reports, artwork, designs for new technology, scientific publications, newspaper stories, editorials, or new case studies. When students review each others' products, they discuss differing methods and results, as is common in scientific discourse.

**ICBL Strategy Box 6** *Be sure to assess all that you want students to learn.* It is well understood that the way students are tested is the most significant factor in how they will approach learning in a course. Be sure to include assessments of the students' skills in identifying questions, resources, investigative methodologies, and values as well as their knowledge of the science concepts. Assessments of process and values can be formal, as illustrated above, or they can include observations of students at work, summaries written by students of the strategies employed by their group, and so forth.

*Examine the following news sources about a chemical spill into the watershed for the town's drinking water supply. Which would you choose to identify the dangers? Why?*

- An article on the web written anonymously and posted on a public bulletin board.
- A newscaster's notes and videotape of interviews with two residents.
- An interview on the radio with a team of scientists from the chemical company.

## Summary

Integrating what students learn in biology with their own interests and concerns enables them to develop an appreciation for the power of science to solve problems. Although there are multiple ways to accomplish this (see, e.g., Tolman, 1999), the *LifeLines OnLine* materials and ICBL strategies described here provide a wealth of resources to these ends.

*LifeLines OnLine* modules and methods offer a reasonable approach to needed reforms to the traditional biology curriculum because students not only identify issues and frame questions of interest to them, but they also learn to locate and manage information, develop reasonable answers to the questions, provide support for their conclusions, and work on decision-making abilities. Some web sites related to *LifeLines OnLine* materials and strategies include the prototype *LifeLines OnLine* web site *(http://bioquest.org/llacube)*, possible initial steps in ICBL *(http://cstl.semo. edu/waterman/LifeLines/zeaim-plement.htm)*, ways in which simulation software might link to a case *(http://bioquest. org/case.html)*, and excerpts from our paper describing the Investigative Case Study Approach for Biology Learning *(http://bioquest.orgcase99.html)*.

We believe that biology learning should result in applicable, flexible knowledge of the living world as well as the ability to investigate biological problems. In order to value a scientific approach to problem-solving in their own lives, students should use scientific reasoning to iden-

tify, explore, and resolve meaningful concerns in the classroom, laboratory, or field.

Case-based learning emphasizes the role of the students in defining not only the problems to be studied, but also in the development of strategies by which to approach these problems. Group work further enhances problem-solving skills by letting students collaborate with their peers and use multiple resources. Lastly, this approach allows students to practice their newly acquired scientific literacy as they support their own conclusions and evaluate those of others.

### Note

*The* LifeLines OnLine *project is supported by the National Science Foundation, Division of Undergraduate Education, Grant No. DUE-9952525.*

### References

American Association of Community Colleges. 1998. National Community College Snapshot. Online at *http://www.aacc.nche.edu/allaboutcc.snapshot.html* accessed 3/99

Arneson, P., and B. E. Ticknor. 1998. Lateblight. In *BioQUEST Library V*, eds. J. R. Jungck and V. Vaughan. New York: Academic Press.

Barrows, H. S., and R. Tamblyn. 1980. *Problem-Based Learning*. New York: Springer.

Cooke, B. P. 1994. Rethinking teaching and testing: Quality in the classroom. Paper presented at the 7th Eastern Regional Competency-Based Education Consortium Conference, Asheville, NC.

Eaton, J. S. 1993. General education in the community college: Developing habits of thought. In *New Directions for Community Colleges*, ed. N.A. Raisman, 81, Spring.

Ercegovac, Z. 1997. The interpretation of library use in the age of digital libraries: Virtualizing the name. *Library & Information Science Research* 19(1): 31-46.

Ercegovak, Z., and E.Yamasaki. 1998. Information literacy: Search strategies, tools and resources. A Digest of the ERIC Clearinghouse for Community Colleges, UCLA.

Ertmer, P. A., and D. R. Dillon. 1998. Shooting in the dark versus breaking it down: Understanding students' approaches to case-based instruction. *Qualitative Studies in Education* 11(4): 605-622.

Finkle, S. L., and L. L. Torp. 1995. Introductory documents. (Available from the Center for Problem-Based Learning, Illinois Math and Science Academy, 1500 West Sullivan Road, Aurora, IL 60506-1000.)

Flynn, W. J. 1998. The search for the learning centered college. In *New Expeditions: Charting the Second Century of Community Colleges*. W.K. Kellogg Foundation. *(Available http://www.aacc.nche.edu/initiatives/new expeditions/)*

Knowles, M. 1984. *Andragogy in Action*. San Francisco: Jossey-Bass.

Herreid, C. F. 1999. St. Anthony and the chicken poop. JCST 29(1): 13-16.

National Science Foundation. 1996. *Shaping the future: New expectations for undergraduate education in science, mathematics, engineering and technology*. Washington, DC. Author. Document 96-139.

Shotwell, R. A. 1996 (May). Scientific literacy: A non-traditional approach to science for students outside of technical fields. Paper presented at the National Institute for Staff and Organizational Development Conference on Teaching and Leadership Excellence, Austin, TX.

Stepien, W., and S. Gallagher. 1993 (April). Problem-based learning: As authentic as it gets. *Educational Leadership*, pp. 25-28.

Stover, D. 1998. Problem-based learning: Redefining self-directed instruction and learning. *Forum* 7(1).

Tolman, D. A. 1999. A science-in-the-making course for nonscience majors. JCST 29(1): 41-46.

Waterman, M. A. 1998. Investigative case study approach for biology learning. *Bioscene: Journal of College Biology Teaching* 24(1): 3-10.

Waterman, M. A., and E. D. Stanley. 1998. Investigative cases and case-based learning in biology. In *BioQUEST Library V*, eds. J. R. Jungck and V. Vaughan, on CD-ROM. New York: Academic Press.

White, R. T. 1988. *Learning Science*. Oxford, UK: Basil Blackwell Ltd.

# Trouble in Paradise

*A Case of Speciation*

JAMES A. HEWLETT

s an expert in the field of mammalian reproductive strategies, you have been hired by the Department of Nature and Island Resources of the West Indies. This organization is a cooperative of several West Indies islands concerned with the loss of biological diversity on their island nations as tourism and development continue to grow. Scientists working on the island of St. Kitts and its sister island Nevis have uncovered what appears to be a previously undiscovered species of rodent.

Based on the original description of this animal, it was placed in a genus within the squirrel family. What you have been hired to do is to help save the population in St. Kitts, which is small and threatened by development. The population is so small that individuals are having difficulty finding mates, and, in many cases, the reproductive seasons are being delayed by up to one year. When you arrive in the region and begin your observations, you notice that the Nevis population is very healthy and could be used as stock for the recovery operation that you plan on the island of St. Kitts.

In your recovery plan, you bring animals from Nevis into the population on St. Kitts to bolster the population numbers, ensure the avail-ability of mates, and increase the genetic diversity within the shrinking population. As a good scientist, you observe the reproductive behaviors of this animal in the field to ensure the success of your program. Within a very short time, you realize that your plan is failing. In the 240 attempts to bring a Nevis animal into the St. Kitts population, you are unable to observe a single successful reproductive event. Although these animals look identical, you are concerned that they are two distinct species. Your focus now becomes identifying the differences between the two populations. See "Data" box for a brief review of the statistics you collected from your study.

## Your assignment

This case study describes a recovery program for a rodent population on the island of St. Kitts in the Caribbean. After reading the case study above, your job is to formulate your own story incorporating some of the details and data provided while also drawing on several evolutionary concepts studied in class. An outline of these topics can be found in the box labeled "Concept List."

There are no limitations on the details you can incorporate into your story, but it should follow some specific guidelines. Your story:
- Should be 600 words or less.

- Should incorporate the data supplied in the case study.
- Should incorporate at least three of the topics from the "Concept List." As you incorporate each concept, you must demonstrate its relevance to your story.
- Can be told in any form. For instance, one student presented the story as field notes collected from observing the animals in their natural habitat. Another student presented the story as a series of experiments and observations made by groups of scientists over hundreds of years. Be creative.
- Will cover very long time periods since it is an evolutionary picture of a species. Keep in mind that in an evolutionary story you will be describing events that may have occurred over very long time periods.
- Should account for the data on the organisms outlined in this case study. It is acceptable to add more data as you develop your story as long as it fits into the patterns of the data provided.
- Can include graphics and illustrations. Be sure to cite the source and give credit for the material, including material taken from the Internet.
- Should include a scientific and common name for the rodent populations. In determining these names, make sure you use the rules for binomial classification. In addition, make sure that you put the rodents into an existing genus. You come up with the species names.
- Needs a good title.

*Important*: When including concepts from the "Concept List" in your story, you must elaborate on how they relate to your story.

Simply including a concept word in your assignment is not acceptable. For example, stating that "the animals became two species because of genetic drift" is not sufficient. You must also explain how genetic drift works in this process.

## Teaching notes

This case study is designed for an introductory biology course or a course on evolution. It is part of a series of cases that carry a similar theme, each with a slightly different story line. This series of cases is part of a contest called "Biolink," which is offered to all General Biology II students at Finger Lakes Community College in Canandaigua, NY. This contest is an annual event that gives students an opportunity to use the principles of evolution learned in class in an open-ended format. Department faculty judge the contest entries, and the winning submission is sent to be professionally mounted as a poster, which is displayed in the hallway of the science and technology department.

There are very few restrictions placed on the format of the submissions, which has led to some very creative contest entries. One student produced what looked like an issue of *Time* magazine, and her story was one of the lead stories (along with a cover shot of the animals). Another student created a laboratory notebook (complete with coffee stains) that documented the findings and field notes as if he were a biologist studying the animals. And another produced an interactive web site complete with maps and graphs.

## Case objectives

By working through this case, the student will:
- have a better understanding of the principles of evolution and classification;
- have a better understanding of the concept of species;
- have a better understanding of the evidence in support of evolution;
- develop a common name for the fictitious species of mammals and apply the rules of binomial classification to provide a scientific name;
- apply concepts of micro- and macro-evolution to produce an evolutionary story for the fictitious mammals;
- interpret simple data sets and make inferences and conclusions from that data; and

---

### Data Collected on Rodent Species

**ST. KITTS RODENT**

Average weight: 83 g

Average length: 21.8 cm

Average hind limb: 7.8 cm

Average forelimb: 4.2 cm

Top speed: 2.2 meters/second (m/s)

Average leap height: 1.4 m

Average gestation time: 29.3 days

Average time spent in courtship display: 12.6 seconds

**NEVIS RODENT**

Average weight: 86 g

Average length: 23.3 cm

Average hind limb: 4.2 cm

Average forelimb: 3.9 cm

Top speed: 0.8 m/s

Average leap height: 0.4 m

Average gestation time: 42.7 days

Average time spent in courtship display: 21.3 seconds

---

- produce data and/or evidence to support an original evolutionary story of the student's own creation.

## Classroom management

The case that was developed for the first trial of the Biolink contest was distributed to the students with the requirement that they produce individual responses (the case involved a population of frogs in Costa Rica). In recent contests, however, including the 1999 contest in which this case was used,

students were encouraged to work in groups. Groups were not allowed to exceed four in size.

The ideal group size for the project is three students. This is the typical lab group size for the biology courses at Finger Lakes Community College. Since the students are already familiar with each other at the time the case is presented in class, we have the lab groups work on the case. Instructors use various methods for establishing lab groups, and, therefore, the selection of the student groups for working with this case also varies.

---

### Concept List

Genetic drift

Bottleneck effect

Founder effect

Gene flow

Mutation

Natural selection - Directional selection

Natural selection - Stabilizing selection

Natural selection - Diversifying selection

Prezygotic reproductive isolation - Habitat isolation

Prezygotic reproductive isolation - Behavioral isolation

Prezygotic reproductive isolation - Temporal isolation

Prezygotic reproductive isolation - Mechanical isolation

Prezygotic reproductive isolation - Genetic isolation

Postzygotic reproductive isolation - Reduced hybrid viability or fertility

Allopatric speciation

---

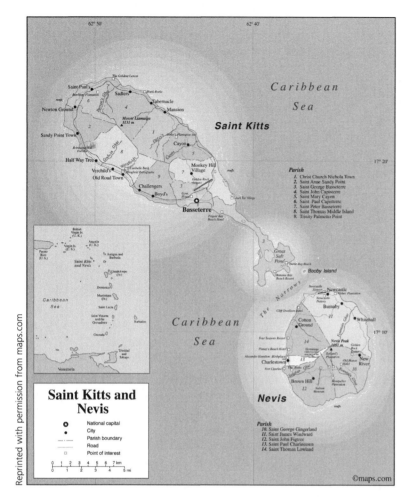

Students have two weeks to produce their responses after the principles of evolution are presented in class. Evolution as a topic is covered in approximately four to five weeks in the General Biology II class at Finger Lakes Community College, and, therefore, the students have the case for approximately six weeks before their responses are due. In the last week of the evolution unit, some time is allocated in class for groups to meet to brainstorm some story ideas. This meeting gives the instructor a chance to interact with the groups and determine the types of stories that are being considered. It will also give the instructor a chance to correct any misconceptions that might have evolved on some of the principles discussed in class. Over the next couple of weeks, students are encouraged to meet outside of class to discuss their case responses and work on the materials they will submit.

### Student preparation

Before students can be expected to produce an original and creative evolutionary story in response to this case, they will need preparation in three main areas: the topics on the "Concept List," the evidence in support of evolution, and the concept of species.

To start, the principles on the concept list should be covered in class. When presenting these concepts, it is a good idea to provide several examples to go along with the basics of each concept. The examples help students think about evolution as a story. Some faculty distribute scientific papers and articles for students to read as a supplement to the classroom activities. If students are exposed to various evolutionary stories before working on the case, they will be better prepared to produce a well-constructed response. The instructor's examples should focus on the evolutionary explanation of very specific traits and behaviors for various organisms. In addition, they should present a mix of micro- and macro-evolutionary principles. Most general biology textbooks offer excellent examples for discussion.

After choosing the principles that they will use and selecting a story line, some groups may decide to produce a story that involves distinct tasks that can be assigned to individual members. A recent example was a submission by a group that included an art major who designed some very creative props to go along with the case submission.

It is a good idea to distribute the case prior to the point in the course where the principles of evolution will be covered. This schedule can enhance student involvement in the classroom discussion of the subject since they will be motivated to ask questions to ensure that they are prepared for the case assignment. If students can see ahead of time that they will need to be able to apply these concepts to the case, they are more likely to be engaged in the classroom and will want to join in the discussion on speciation.

Students will also need to review a wide variety of evidence in support of evolution. When students produce their evolutionary stories, they have to support their stories with valid evidence. To ensure their success in this endeavor, students must be familiar with the following areas tied to evolution:

- Biogeography—the geographical distribution of species. This should include a basic understanding of how islands can be formed (e.g., volcanic origin and uplift).
- The fossil record—the succession of fossil forms and their relationship to contemporaries
- Comparative anatomy
- Comparative embryology
- Molecular biology

Finally, students will need to have an understanding of the concept of species. I employ Ernst Mayr's 1942 biological species concept for discussion. According to the case study, repeated attempts at mating individuals from the two populations is not successful. This often leads students to the idea that the two populations represent two different but closely related species in the same genus. Students are not forced to draw this conclusion. In fact, one student included an artificial means of fertilization in his story, which led to the production of viable offspring. He went on to explain their physical differences, but also included some strong arguments for the possibility that these are not two separate species.

To see examples of several student papers done for this case study, go to the online case collection of the National Center for Case Study Teaching in Science at: *http://ublib.buffalo.edu/libraries/projects/cases/ubcase.htm*.

# A Computerized Approach to Mastery Learning

*Helping Community College
Students Make the Grade in
Anatomy*

KEN GARVER

course in human anatomy is a standard component of many basic health science programs. It is also notorious among students for the work it requires—thousands of different body parts must be learned in the course of a semester. The difficulty level is typically reflected in a high dropout rate and a wide grade distribution.

Over the past few years, we have been working to improve the outcomes in our human anatomy classes at Victor Valley College. These efforts are now bearing fruit, as indicated by dramatically improved test scores and class grades. The key element in this success, we believe, has been to substitute a computerized mastery learning component for some of the traditional lecture sessions and tests.

The conventional approach to teaching anatomy is to try to cover all the course material in lecture. This is often considered necessary because student comprehension of reading assignments is poor. In fact, in many cases, students simply devote insufficient time to studying, hoping to fill in the gaps from lecture. This is where we think computerized quizzing and testing has solved a problem. Student comprehension of reading assignments has improved greatly, en-

abling us to reduce the amount of lecture by approximately one-half. Class time is now devoted primarily to covering difficult concepts and answering questions, and the time that used to be spent on textbook-repetitive lecture is available for the students to spend reviewing and studying for the next day's assignment.

Here is how our system works. Forty percent of a student's grade is based on computerized tests, 15 percent on traditional paper and pencil tests, and 45 percent on labs. Before any evaluations take place, however, students are assigned to read a section of the textbook and take a computerized practice quiz.

These quizzes are quite unlike traditional tests. On a practice quiz, any time students answer a question incorrectly, the computer gives them immediate feedback on their mistake. The quizzes can also be repeated as many times as the students wish, and we recommend that they repeat the quizzes until they reach a level of at least 85 percent. Since the computer selects different questions on the same topics each time a quiz is repeated, this does not become an exercise in rote memorization.

The practice quizzes are related to both the in-class and computerized tests that form part of the student's grade. In both cases, students know that the tests will cover precisely the same topics as the practice quizzes. (They may sometimes contain overlapping questions since the computer is randomly selecting from the same area of a large question database, but with a database of nearly 10,000 questions, the percentage of repeated items is not significant.)

The in-class tests follow the traditional model, with no opportunity to repeat for a better score. The computer tests, by contrast, combine some elements of traditional testing and some elements of mastery learning. Unlike the practice quizzes, there is no immediate feedback on wrong answers; but after the test, students are shown a list of topics where errors occurred, along with their scores. If they are dissatisfied with their score, they can have two more opportunities to improve on it. To enforce the importance of improvement through studying, they must wait at least two days before attempting a repeat. In the meanwhile, students can revisit the practice quizzes if desired. When they retake a test, the computer once again selects a fresh set of questions from the database.

The net result of this system is a much stronger set of incentives than traditional course design provides. In the standard read, lecture, and test approach, students are often left guessing how the course content will be reflected in test questions. Our practice quizzes provide a bridge between course content and tests. Because they are seeing something like the questions they will ultimately have to answer, students are motivated to pay close attention. This makes the tutorials that appear immediately after incorrect answers in practice quizzes even more effective.

The other great motivator is the opportunity to learn from mistakes without penalty. Of course, even in traditional course design, it is always possible to get a better score on a final exam by learning from one's mistakes on a midterm, but in most conventional scoring systems, a low score that reflects a learning experience will still drag down the overall grade average.

In a mastery learning approach, by contrast, students who take the responsibility of learning from their mistakes can get the full reward for their efforts. There is no penalty against their overall score. Student comments make it clear that this is an extremely strong incentive.

Of course, the bottom line for any educational method is the results it produces. We do not have a controlled study on which to base any conclusions, but what we can say is this: since implementing our system of computerized practice quizzes and repeatable computer tests, we have seen an increase of approximately one full grade level in the average class grade. This makes sense, because when we analyze student performance on a test that is taken for the second time, the average improvement is 8.7 percent (with another 6.4 percent improvement if a third attempt is made.) These statistics are based on five sections per class over two semesters since we fully implemented the new system.

Some educators will disagree with our approach. After all, they will say, it is no miracle that scores improve if students are allowed to repeat tests on subjects in which they have previously gotten poor scores. We agree that it is no miracle, but to us the important thing is that students apparently have at least 10 percent better command of the material at the end of the course. Isn't better comprehension the ultimate purpose of education?

We believe that the software we are using has had a lot to do with our success. We began assembling a systematic question database about five years ago using a product called The Question Bank (developed by Teaching Technologies, 3889 N. Van Ness Blvd., Fresno CA 93704.) Question Bank was particularly useful for our purposes because: it has strong graphics capability (very important for the many questions that include anatomical drawings), and it has an integrated outlining system that enabled us to classify our questions very specifically by topic so we could create several tests covering the very same topics in each area of the course. Eventually, we assembled a very large database of anatomy questions.

More recently, Teaching Technologies introduced PC University, a package that has enabled us to use our question database (including all our graphics) for on-line mastery quizzing and testing. As far as we know, PC University is unique in its ability to present on-line tests either with immediate feedback (as we do during our practice quizzes) or with no feedback until the end of the test (as in our computer tests.) PCU also contains a number of other tools that are useful to us: it enables us to record and link the "help screens" that appear when students answer questions incorrectly, it keeps track of our specified "mastery levels" and won't allow a student to proceed from one quiz to another unless the mastery level has been reached, and it has a very good set of randomizing mechanisms so that when students retake quizzes, they are not just memorizing the same set of questions.

Unlike some of the other "drill and practice" packages we looked at, PCU seems to have been genuinely designed for mastery learning purposes.

The distinction between mere drill and practice and the kind of retesting that takes place in a mastery learning environment is important to emphasize. Many educational computing gurus automatically dismiss any kind of computerized quizzing and testing as "drill and kill." What these critics fail to see is the value of combining computer quizzing with mastery learning. Of course, if all that computerized quizzing amounts to is factoring the results from old-fashioned no-feedback testing into a traditional grade average, it is not going to inspire many students. But our approach has been quite different.

In short, if our students are being "killed" by computerized quizzing and testing, they are certainly enjoying their death. In the most recent set of course evaluations, over 90 percent of the students indicated that they would like the opportunity to take another course with a computerized mastery learning component. An astonishing 98.5 percent expressed a favorable opinion of mastery learning and said they thought it had increased their understanding and retention of the course material.

Based on both subjective and objective evidence, we believe that computerized mastery learning has the potential to dramatically transform the educational landscape.

**Note**

*For further information on the above-mentioned software, please contact Teaching Technologies, 3889 N. Van Ness Boulevard, Fresno, CA 93704; tel: 209-222-7879, Fax: 209-222-7879.*

# Screening Prospective Laboratory Telecourse Students

*Eliminating the Negative to Accentuate the Positive in Distance Learning*

ROBERT L. WARASILA AND GEORGE S. LOMAGA

uffolk County Community College (SCCC) is a multi-campus institution serving approximately 20,000 students in a suburban environment east of New York City. This fall, SCCC is offering 22 sections of distance learning (DL) courses, most of which are presented in the telecourse mode. In a telecourse, students watch videotapes in place of listening to lectures. The instructor provides a detailed set of "learning guides" that integrate assignments based on the tapes, text, questions from the text, and a series of paper-based lab exercises.

We are now expanding the DL program by introducing online courses under the auspices of the State University of New York Learning Net. Our DL program is featured on the web site: *http://www.sunysuffolk.edu/Web/VirtualCampus.* This paper deals with our experience teaching lab science as a telecourse and particularly with the screening process we used to identify and counsel students who are best suited to this learning modality. Some students are not suited to DL because they aren't mature enough to schedule their own study time or they do not like to work

independently. Such students benefit more from the lecture and question/answer process that occurs in a traditional classroom.

## The science telecourses

We have offered three different science telecourses to date: Physical Geology (ES15), Astronomy of the Solar System (ES21), and Astronomy of the Stars and Galaxies (ES22). ES15 was the first course available, starting about eight years ago. It is currently designed around the textbook series *The Earth Revealed*.

After Coastline Community College released the videotape *Universe: The Infinite Frontier* five years ago, our astronomy lab materials, published as *Astronomy Through Practical Investigations,* were selected as the recommended materials for the series, supplementing Michael Seed's *Horizons, Exploring the Universe.* With this encouragement, we decided to offer a section of both astronomy courses in the telecourse mode in addition to the ES15.

All three lab science courses meet for three hours of lecture and two hours of lab a week in the traditional format. When we first introduced ES15 as a telecourse, we met with the students

## WEB SITE SELF-TEST

Suffolk County Community College offers distance-education classes including online courses and telecourses. These classes are not for everyone. How well would distance-education courses fit your circumstances and lifestyle? For each question in the quiz below select one answer and click the radio button for your response. Your answers will be evaluated when you click on "Submit" at the bottom of the page.

- **My need to take this course now is:**
1. high - I need it immediately for a degree, job, or other important reason.
2. moderate - I could take it on campus later or substitute another course.
3. low - it's a personal interest that could be postponed.

- **Feeling that I am part of a class is:**
1. not particularly necessary to me.
2. somewhat important to me.
3. very important to me.

- **I would classify myself as someone who:**
1. often gets things done ahead of time.
2. needs reminding to get things done on time.
3. puts things off until the last minute.

- **Classroom discussion is:**
1. rarely helpful to me.
2. sometimes helpful to me.
3. almost always helpful to me.

- **When an instructor hands out directions for an assignment, I prefer:**
1. figuring out the instructions myself.
2. trying to follow the directions on my own, then asking for help as needed.
3. having the instructions explained to me.

- **I need faculty comments on my assignments:**
1. within a few weeks so I can review what I did.
2. within a few days or I forget what I did.
3. right away or I get very frustrated.

- **Considering my professional and personal schedule, the amount of time I have to work on a distance-education course is:**
1. more than enough for a campus class or a distance-education course.
2. the same as for a class on campus.
3. less than for a class on campus.

- **When I am asked to use VCRs, computers, email, or other technologies new to me:**
1. I look forward to learning new skills.
2. I feel apprehensive but try anyway.
3. I put it off or try to avoid it.

- **As a reader, I would classify myself as:**
1. good - I usually understand the text without help.
2. average - I sometimes need help to understand the text.
3. slower than average.

- **If I have to go to campus to take exams or complete work:**
1. I can go to campus anytime.
2. I might miss some lab assignments or exam deadlines if campus labs are not open evenings and weekends.
3. I will have difficulty getting to the campus, even in the evenings and on weekends.

- **The VCR, TV, or computer equipment required for the class:**
1. is at home, at work, or somewhere else that is readily available to me.
2. may be difficult at times to locate.
3. is not readily available to me.

- **When it comes to the organization of the class material:**
1. I can learn even if the class is not highly structured.
2. I like some structure in the course.
3. I have difficulty learning when a class is not highly structured.

\* \* \*

A student who checks choice #1 for each question receives this recommendation from the system: *"You are likely to be successful taking a distance-learning class. Regardless of your score we recommend that you discuss this survey with a counselor."*

for three to five three-hour sessions, which was standard practice at our college for the three-credit liberal arts telecourses. We quickly decided that a lab science course requires more contact and changed to a format of seven four-hour sessions. Most of the time spent in these sessions is devoted to lab activities and testing; ES15 also includes a field trip to examine local geological features.

Although 28 contact hours may seem to contradict the distance-learning concept, it has been our experience that this time is necessary for the student population we serve. The students generally are appreciative of this support and of the fact that they still enjoy far more flexibility in scheduling than they would in the traditional format. All our sessions meet in the evenings and/or on Saturdays to reach out to students with busy schedules. All SCCC lab science courses are restricted to 24-seat enrollments and have an elementary algebra prerequisite that is strictly enforced. Almost all our science courses are taught with a required lab.

Since all liberal arts and sciences curricula require at least one laboratory science course, we have a steady population of nonmajors. Our laboratory earth science telecourses recently have attracted students seeking teaching certification in the earth sciences because of the shortage of certified teachers in this area. Although we have always seen this group in our evening offerings, they are more pronounced in the telecourses because of the flexibility of the schedule.

## Counseling deficiency

To date we have offered approximately 25 sections of ES15, ES21 and ES22 in the telecourse format. In the 1998-99 academic year, we started worrying about the success rate of students in these courses and soon after began to explore the efficacy of screening registrants for the special study skills these courses demand. Our intent was to determine whether this additional screening effort, supplementing the existing counseling program, would enhance student success with the coursework.

At that point, our counseling of registrants included a variety of supportive approaches. The SCCC Distance Learning web site offered a self-test to help students determine their suitability for distance learning (see "Web Site Self-Test"). In a more targeted approach, we required instructors to contact telecourse students a few weeks before the semester begins to orient them to the special challenges of this format. In addition, we reiterated these points, especially as they apply to a lab science course, at the first class meeting. It was apparent, however, that these counseling measures, without systematic screening, were relatively ineffective.

In fact, not all registrants received this counseling. At the beginning of the timeframe covered by our study, SCCC students could register for courses in person or by telephone. Now they can also register online. If this is not their first semester and they are students in good standing, they can register without first obtaining counseling, to say nothing of screening. The college implemented this process in order to present a more "customer friendly" environment. In our view, it is not good practice, and we proceeded to initiate and develop our screening program. At the same time, we began compiling data to compare screened and nonscreened sections of the ES15 and ES21 courses (see Tables 1 and 2).

## The screening process

The screening process required all students who tried to register for a science telecourse to be interviewed. We facilitated the process by employing a computer block that prohibited direct student registration for these courses. A few cases of senior administrators overriding the block were encountered, but the vast majority of students (>98 percent) were interviewed before being enrolled.

Starting with the summer 1999 semester, one of us (RLW) volunteered to screen all science telecourse applicants before placing them. The interviewer was accessible by phone, e-mail, and in person. The printed schedule and online sched-

**Table 1.**
Grade distributions for nonscreened sections

| Grade | ES15 Physical Geology | | ES21 Solar System Astronomy | |
|---|---|---|---|---|
| A | 8 | 12% | 5 | 8% |
| B+ | 9 | 13% | 6 | 10% |
| B | 7 | 10% | 4 | 7% |
| C+ | 2 | 3% | 6 | 10% |
| C | 7 | 10% | 9 | 15% |
| D+ | 3 | 4% | 2 | 3% |
| D | 4 | 6% | 5 | 8% |
| F | 11 | 16% | 1 | 2% |
| INC | 6 | 9% | 4 | 7% |
| W | 12 | 17% | 19 | 31% |
| **Totals** | **69** | | **61** | |

**Table 2.**
Grade distributions for screened sections

| Grade | ES15 Physical Geology | | ES21 Solar System  Astronomy | |
|---|---|---|---|---|
| A | 10 | 22% | 10 | 31% |
| B+ | 6 | 13% | 4 | 13% |
| B | 7 | 15% | 3 | 9% |
| C+ | 4 | 9% | 3 | 9% |
| C | 7 | 15% | 5 | 16% |
| D+ | 3 | 7% | 1 | 3% |
| D | 1 | 2% | 2 | 6% |
| F | 1 | 2% | 1 | 3% |
| INC | 0 | 0% | 0 | 0% |
| W | 7 | 15% | 3 | 9% |
| **Totals** | **46** | | **32** | |

ule carried the contact information and emphasized that an interview was required for registration in these particular sections. Largely because of the support of the computer systems staff the process worked well. It is clear, however, that the screening process does lose students who do not want to participate in the screening and who, had they participated, might have been successful in the telecourses. On the other hand, we suspect that unwillingness to expend the effort required by the screening process selectively eliminates some students who are not sufficiently motivated to seriously engage in distance learning.

The interview process consisted of obtaining data from student transcripts as well as from discussions with the prospective enrollees. We first ascertained that the students satisfied the algebra prerequisite for a lab science course and appraised their general academic success based on GPA and courses attempted, especially courses of a quantitative nature. Furthermore, we asked the interviewees about their previous experience with telecourses and their comfort level with science courses in general.

We presented several caveats: we warned students about the independent study and self-discipline they would need to succeed as distance learners, we reminded them how supportive interaction with other students and the instructor in the classroom can be, and we emphasized that this teaching and learning modality is probably the most difficult way to satisfy the lab science course requirement. If at that point the student still wished to enroll, we added him or her to the roster and reiterated that the instructor would be in contact before the class began.

## Results and observations

Tables 1 and 2 show the data for the 10 sections of telecourses we have offered from fall 1998 to summer 2000. During this period, five sections each of ES15 and ES21 were offered; three were nonscreened and two were screened. The spring semester of the 1999-00 academic year was not screened because of an administrative oversight. The sections in this nonscreened semester did as poorly as earlier nonscreened groups. The ES15 students were taught by one of us (GSL), and all but one ES21 section was taught by the other author. The data tables show that nonscreened and screened outcomes differ principally in the F/INC/W grade group: these grades were significantly reduced in the screened population.

There are other trends in the data, but at this point there are insufficient numbers upon which to base additional conclusions.

In any event, we believe that our screening process, still in the evolving stage, shows promise as an effective tool for supplementing counseling and enhancing students success with DL coursework.

We offer the following observations:

- Using the criterion that a course grade of C is required for course transferability, the screened group does much better than the nonscreened group at transferring these courses to a four-year school.
- The principal problem in the nonscreened group is reflected in the F/INC/W grades, which identify students who could not complete the course. Because of the grading criteria used, we can reasonably assume F and W grades to be equivalent in most cases. About 20 percent of the INC were eventually converted to passing grades.
- The screening process appears to have resulted in more students registering for the physical geology (ES15) class than the astronomy class. That was not a deliberate placement bias, but during the interview if students asked, "Which course is easier?", we told them that the geology course was more descriptive than the astronomy offerings. Although the distribution from A to C differed for the two courses in the nonscreened group, the totals were the same. This suggests that the courses present equal difficulty to a nonscreened enrollee.
- When two sections were offered, the screening process appears to have decreased the total enrollment. This raises a philosophical issue regarding the role of good advisement. That is, do we owe students the right to register for a course when it is likely they will not finish it, or do we block them from enrolling at the expense of having to run smaller—and therefore more expensive—sections. Ordinarily in the sciences, we rely on prerequisites to provide this screening; however, in the DL

arena, the student's independent study skills are of equal importance.

- We believe the high percentage of As and B+s reflects the popularity of these courses with students who are seeking earth science certification.

## Conclusion

We are still in the early stages of the screening process, but so far it has greatly improved the course success rate of students and opened up seats for students who previously were "locked out" by enrollees who were unsuited to the DL modality. If we functioned in an environment where all students were required to meet with an advisor before registering for courses, this procedure might not be necessary. The reality in many institutions, however, is that students frequently "place" themselves into courses they are likely to fail. They do this largely out of ignorance of what will be required of them and whether they are suited to that requirement. Economic considerations pressure us to "fill seats," but conscience should require us to steer students into classroom environments where they have a good chance of success.

## Note

*SUNY Learning Net is a collaborative effort of the institutions that make up the State University of New York (SUNY). This includes university centers, four-year units, and community colleges. Almost every campus has contributed one or more sources to an online learning offering sponsored by the SUNY System Administration, Office of the Provost, Advanced Learning & Information Services. The extent and spirit of the program can be found at:* http://sln.suny.edu/admin/sln/original/nsf.

## References

*The Earth Revealed.* 1992. Washington, D.C.: Annenberg/CPB Foundation.

Lomaga, G., W. Smiley, and R. Warasila. 1987-97. *Astronomy Through Practical Investigations, Selected Topics.* Brantingham, NY: L.S.W. Publications.

Seeds, M. A. 2000. *Horizons: Exploring the Universe.* Pacific Grove, CA: Brooks/Cole.

*Universe: The Infinite Frontier.* 1995. Fountain Valley, CA: Coast Telecourses, Coastline Community College.

# Teaching Introductory Agriculture Courses Through Distance Education Technology at Louisiana State University

BRUNO BORSARI

istance education is the method of teaching and learning across a physical distance between the instructor and the student (Muggli-Cocket et al., 1992). The feasibility and efficacy of this innovative technology have already been amply demonstrated in different educational and training sectors.

The implementation of agricultural courses through distance education technology seems also to be very attractive to many land grant universities. Many students interested in agriculture come from rural areas that are often poorly served in terms of quality education, and enrollment in colleges of agriculture have suffered in recent years despite growing opportunities for college graduates in the food and agricultural sciences.

There is no reassuring evidence on the horizon that either of these trends will be reversed in the coming years. Thus the future well-being of academic programs, the assignment of faculty to them, and resource allocations from main campuses to their colleges are increasingly jeopardized (Russell, 1993).

The growing interest in distance education technology from many colleges of agriculture is more than legitimate. Attracting new students to these curricula to remedy the current decline in enrollment could be listed as the primary justification for rapidly introducing this technology. Even though distance education is still a controversial topic in higher education, evidence shows clearly that its implementation is unavoidable, as Jacobson pointed out in 1994. However, many skeptics still exist especially among faculty members who may see this educational revolution as a potential threat to their job security (Blumenstyck, 1994).

Historically, distance education in agriculture has been in place for a long time. Pennsylvania State College (today Pennsylvania State University) began a correspondence program in agriculture in 1892. Two years later, the institution's annual report described the program as a home reading program modeled after the Chautauqua approach (Miller, 1995).

With the objective of rejuvenating interest in agricultural sciences and attracting students who normally live far away from the main campus, an introductory course in animal science

(ANSC 1011) was delivered to the LSU-Eunice campus (a two-year college) from LSU-Baton Rouge, in the fall semester, 1996. The course targeted freshmen and sophomore students without any previous formal education in this discipline. Its design reflected the general philosophy of E.B. Russell (1993) who stated: "How youth development is viewed and addressed will have a fundamental effect on youth as well as the educational programs designed for them." This opportunity allowed students of the Eunice area to enroll and pursue college credit for a course that otherwise should have been attended on the main campus, approximately 80 miles away from this rural community.

## Course development

Carefully planning a distance education course well in advance is fundamental to the success of the course. Starting early is a key to making things work. As explained by Nichols and Trout (1994):

> Beginning the planning process one year in advance of the actual course was [the] optimal [situation]. Advanced planning allowed [the authors] to meet catalog and time schedule printing deadlines at both universities and do publicity [of their own] at the branch campuses where the course would be down linked.

And, too, early planning allows sufficient time for course developers to get valuable input from faculty members and the technical staff.

In this case, for example, advanced planning allowed us to prepare an extended syllabus for this ANSC 1011 to support the distance learners independent work more effectively. It contained detailed learning objectives, a glossary, a bibliography for supplemental reading, and home assignments. We also developed and compiled videotape segments, slides, and computer generated graphics before the class began. Sufficient lead time allowed colleagues within the department of animal science to review and critique these

materials, which resulted in the refinement and selection of the most appropriate teaching tools for the course.

In order to promote interaction between individual students, the instructor, and the instructional sites, we made fax machines easily available. And the touch-tone microphones on students' and the instructor's desks provided a good means of direct communication.

Less personal contact with students has potential for creating some problems that need to be addressed. Class attendance at distant sites can be difficult to control unless special attention is paid to it. Students need to know that attendance is a factor influencing academic success and that the classroom teacher will monitor it. Giving extra points for class participation improves attendance. And firm dates for handing in assignments with loss of points for each day of delay will minimize student procrastination (Muggli-Cockett et al., 1992).

The instructor also felt some occasional difficulty with stimulating students at the distant site into active discussion. Many trainees are reluctant to ask a question of a classroom teacher, much less of a TV instructor. To minimize such reluctance, instructors can design their classes in a way to minimize students' stressful interactions through the audio link (Shepard, 1992). Television can be an extremely effective delivery medium if the instructor is adequately prepared for the culture shock that usually accompanies a broadcast. Proper support from the television technical staff, absolute mastery of the material, and familiarity with the technology of the "electronic classroom" are essential (Shepard, 1992).

## Evaluation

We conducted a summative course evaluation just before the final exam. This evaluation was solicited from the LSU-Eunice students to appraise the quality of the course they had just completed. Ten core questions asked the students to evaluate the course (objectives, grading procedure, and testing skills assessment) and the instructor (delivery of the course materials, availability, teaching effectiveness, use of instructional media). Five more questions were specifically related to evaluating the lecture (effective use of time, encouragement of student participation, the textbook, and the instructor's enthusiasm and interest).

Sixteen LSU-Eunice students participated in the evaluation. The average overall rating of the class was ($\bar{x}\pm SD$) $4.59\pm0.66$ (on a 5.0 scale) for the core questions and ($\bar{x}\pm SD$) $4.48\pm0.74$ for the lecture evaluation. Three students (19 percent) commented that they had difficulty enjoying the course, but their written remarks were inconsistent with the high grades they gave to the core questions.

The course evaluation demonstrated the success of the initiative, but it would be more appropriate to design a different questionnaire, one that includes questions that specifically address the broadcast medium for this kind of course. It would also be useful to include evaluations of the proctors at the receiving sites and the instructor's remarks for a more valid evaluation of distance education courses.

## Advantages and disadvantages

Distance education provides several potential benefits to the students. Chief among them is the improvement in instructional quality. A wide variety of instructional techniques are used to enrich these courses including computer generated graphics, videotape segments, video stills, guest lecturers and interviews, and an extended syllabus.

Distance education also has disadvantages. The technology involved inflates the cost of producing a distance education course regardless of the numbers of students enrolled in the class. In addition, these courses require considerable instructor effort in their preparation. The increased effort is unavoidable, but the burden on the instructor can be lessened by assigning tasks to other people involved in the course development (Muggli-Cockett et al., 1992).

There are several approaches to supplementing a course with practical laboratory classes and hands-on work. Kennepohl and Last (1997) describe their experience in teaching laboratories that accompany distance education courses. These authors explain:

At Athabasca University (AU), Canada's open university, we use a number of approaches to laboratory work, including home lab kits, residential schools, the use of laboratories in regional centers, and computer simulations, and we frequently use more than one approach in any given course. The goal in using such methods would not be to replace laboratory work with simulated experiments, but rather to provide the student with a better idea of what to expect on entering the laboratory.

## Conclusions

Distance learning does bring knowledge to those who need it in a convenient and cost-effective manner. The flexibility and responsiveness of this learning medium allow learners in any environment to access information that can be directly applied to social, educational, or work dynamics.

Prior to accepting the telecourse format as a viable method of instruction, faculty and administrators must recognize its opportunities and options as well as its limitations and differences from a traditional classroom model of instruction (Klinger, 1992). It is important, as many institutions moving into distance learning programs have discovered, to offer training, support, and incentive that encourages faculty participation. With proper institutional support, the incentives, resources, and ongoing encouragement can strengthen initiatives and build toward their combined success (Klinger, 1992).

For the LSU College of Agriculture, the implementation of more introductory courses will entail several advantages. Agriculture students will be able to enroll in these courses at satellite campuses, like LSU-Eunice, with considerable economic advantages for them and these remote institutions as well. The college at the distant site will be able to retain students more easily and to prepare them properly for their transfer to the main campus. And, upon transferring, the students will be eligible for the advanced courses in their curriculum.

### References

Ball, J. 1994. Texas facility serves as a hub for distance learning. *T.H.E. Journal* (December): 64-68.

Blumenstyk, G. 1994. Networks to the rescue? Using telecommunications networks to serve more students without the costs of building a new campus. *Chronicle of Higher Education* 8(1): 35-39.

Brigham, D. E. 1992. Factors affecting the development of distance education. *Distance Education* 13(2): 169-192.

Jacobson, R. L. 1994. Extending the reach of "virtual" classrooms. *Chronicle of Higher Education* (July 6):A19-21.

Jackson, W. 1985. *New Roots for Agriculture.* Lincoln: University of Nebraska Press.

Kennepohl, D., and A. M. Last. 1997. Science at a distance. *Journal of College Science Teaching* 27(1): 35-38.

Klinger, T. H. 1992. Designing distance learning courses for critical thinking. *T.H.E. Journal* (October): 20, 87-89.

Muggli-Cocket, N. E., J. C. Christensen, R. L. Boman. 1992. Preparing and implementing an animal science course for distance education at Utah State University. *Journal of Dairy Science* 75(November): 3257-60.

Nichols, L. A. S., and M. J. Trout. 1994. Team teaching via two-way interactive video. *The Agricultural Education Magazine* (February): 10-11, 66.

Russell, E. B. 1993. Attracting youth to agriculture. How colleges of agriculture can expand their role. *Journal of Extension* (Winter): 13-14.

Shepard, S. 1992, TV training tips. *Training and Development* (February): 46, 56.

# Introductory Biology *Online*

## *Assessing Outcomes of Two Student Populations*

MARGARET JOHNSON

Peter Drucker, the legendary philosopher of corporate management, has an uncanny knack for predicting the future. Recently Drucker predicted the demise of traditional college education, which he sees as inefficient and overpriced (Bray, 1999). "Universities won't survive. The future is outside the traditional campus. Distance learning is coming on fast."

Soaring student demand for distance-education classes lends credence to Drucker's prediction. InterEd, an Arizona-based research firm, estimated that in 1997, a million students were taking classes online, while 13 million students enrolled in traditional classes (Bray, 1999). InterEd estimates the number of online students will triple in three short years. At our own campus (Mesa Community College), the number of distance-education students quadrupled in two short years, increasing from 424 students in the fall of 1998 to 1745 students in the fall of 2000.

Some educators and community leaders are distressed at the emergence of this new mode of instruction. Historian David F. Noble states that "students want the genuine face-to-face education they paid for, not a cyber-counterfeit" (1998).

In hearings conducted in May 2000, Nick Smith, chairman of the House of Representatives science subcommittee on basic research, expressed deep concerns about the quality of online courses (Carnevale 2000). Believing online students suffer from a "lack of socialization" in their courses, Smith suggested further assessment is needed.

> *Outcomes assessments were conducted with a pretest/post-test design in an online non-majors' biology course that included laboratory and lecture components. Data were compared with those of students at the same college enrolled in the same course with the same instructor on-campus. No significant differences were found in outcomes for students in the two modes of instruction.*

Before we make the commitment to invest considerably more time, financial resources, and technological expertise in developing online courses, it is imperative that we assess whether this mode of instruction can deliver. We need to know if students can satisfactorily achieve learning objectives in an online class.

The learning objectives for an introductory biology course include the ability to apply scientific reasoning skills; store, retrieve, and interpret data using standard graphing techniques; design controlled experiments; and identify causal relationships between independent and dependent variables. Can an online biology course facilitate these objectives? Can students be given the opportunity to "do science" online, rather than just read about or simulate experiments? The results of a study that addresses these questions follow.

## The inquiry approach

Bio 100 online is a nonmajors' biology course that incorporates hands-on, inquiry-based labs that students conduct at home. Students purchase kits containing supplies needed to conduct activities described in a hard-copy lab manual. Some labs also require purchases at the local store (e.g., ammonia, acetone [fingernail polish remover], etc.).

A new experiment is conducted at the beginning of each of 14 weeks (Fig. 1). Based on the learning cycle method of instruction (Karplus, 1977; Lawson, 1988), new concepts are introduced to students in lab. Most explorations begin with a causal question and ask the student to develop alternative hypotheses. Weekly online bulletin board postings (asynchronous) require each student to describe an experiment he or she designed and implemented that addressed the causal question posed for the week. Discussion follows, eliciting feedback from other students and the instructor as to whether or not variables were adequately controlled. (Go to *JCST's* website at *www.nsta.org* to see examples of electronic discussions between students and instruc-

**Figure 1.**
Online laboratory activities

- What factors affect the behavior of animals?
- What factors affect heart rate?
- Where should brine shrimp lay their eggs?
- When do atoms bond together to make molecules?
- What are organic substances like?
- What factors affect reaction rates?
- Getting to know plants up close and personally.
- What factors affect the rate at which organisms get energy from food?
- What factors affect what gets in and out of cells?
- Can we predict what the offspring will look like if we know the parents?
- How do cells reproduce?
- What causes species to change over time?
- What causes changes in chromosome number?
- How are organisms grouped and identified?

tor.) Students discuss the appropriate conclusion as to whether or not the evidence indicates a causal relationship between the independent and dependent variables that were explored.

Students frequently graph their data and submit them to the instructor. Some assignments (such as a chromatogram) are also mailed to the instructor.

One lab asks students to investigate what factors affect the rate of diffusion of substances into cells. Students make Knox® gelatin cubes of various sizes. The liquid they use to dissolve the gelatin is obtained by boiling purple cabbage in water. The anthocyanin pigments thus extracted from the cabbage act as a pH indicator. The student observes the rate of color change in the various cubes as acidic or basic substances diffuse into the cubes. When asked to describe their experimental design and their results on the online class bulletin board, students note the rate of diffusion is much faster in smaller cubes than in larger cubes. This leads to a discussion of the surface area—volume ratio in which students and instructor participate. Figure 1 includes a complete list of online lab activities. These approximate, as much as possible, lab activities performed by on-campus Bio 100 students.

When students need to view images with a microscope, high-resolution micrographs of the appropriate organisms/structures are provided online (e.g., amoeba, cells undergoing mitosis). I believe the microscope is simply a tool to make small entities visible, much like viewing a video of marine animals to see what they look like without ever going deep-sea diving. If a student elects later on to become a biology major, then the microscope is a tool with which they must become skilled. They will have many opportunities to do so in their subsequent coursework

Students also read the textbook *The Unity and Diversity of Life* (8th ed., by Starr and Taggart, Wadsworth Publishing) and complete online modules using WebCT® software. Modules are equivalent to on-campus lectures, but are structured in a question-and-answer format to keep students actively involved. Some modules incorporate the use of a CD-ROM that accompanies the textbook, providing animations of selected abstract concepts.

Students take a weekly online quiz. If they have not completed the week's assignments before taking the quiz, there is insufficient time to assimilate and apply the concepts successfully on the quiz. Students receive the graded quiz back along with the reason an answer was incorrect. The quiz is an important evaluation tool that alerts the student as to what concepts need more work. The majority of the course grade (60 percent) is determined by performance on a proctored midterm and comprehensive final examination.

Assessment is a key course component. In this study, outcomes were assessed for two subsequent semesters of online Bio 100 (N = 34 for the first semester and N=32 for the second semester). Us-

ing the same instruments, results were compared with an on-campus class of Bio 100 (N=50) taught by the same instructor in a previous semester.

On-campus Bio 100 students were taught with the inquiry approach for similar content in laboratory and lecture classes. Both online and on-campus classes explored such topics as atomic structure, water, chemical bonds, macromolecules, osmosis, photosynthesis, cellular respiration, cell division, DNA, Mendelian genetics, and population dynamics. However, on-campus students did use a different textbook, *Understanding Biology* by Raven and Johnson (2nd edition, Mosby Publishing Company).

Students were pre- and post-tested for knowledge of biology, graphing skills, reasoning ability, and attitudes toward science. Data were also gathered on four descriptive variables: number of previous biology courses completed, race, age, and gender. Withdrawal rates were tabulated. Results were analyzed by a Chi square test and/or analysis of variance.

## Measures of learning objectives

### Knowledge of biology
The pretest of biology concepts was constructed from test banks accompanying introductory nonmajors' college biology textbooks. Mean scores for the pretest on biology concepts correlated positively with the number of previous biology classes subjects had completed.

Students were post-tested for knowledge of biology using 50 multiple-choice questions from the 80 questions that constituted the 1987 National Association of Biology Teachers/National Science Teachers Association High School Biology Examination. The 50 multiple-choice questions were selected by a science educator who had demonstrated, through his investigations and publications, a good understanding of both Piagetian theory and the discipline of biology. The instructor involved in this study did not see the examination at any time during the study and thus was not able to "teach to the test."

### Reasoning levels

Reasoning levels were determined using a slightly modified version of the Lawson Classroom Test of Scientific Reasoning which has been found to have face validity, convergent validity, and factorial validity (Lawson, 1978, 1987). Students are classified as to their Piagetian reasoning category: concrete (can reason with visible objects), transitional (can reason abstractly in some contexts), or formal (can reason abstractly with many or most contexts). Twelve multiple-choice questions were presented in a paper-and-pencil format for on-campus students (Johnson 1993). Online students answered the same questions online. Each question was followed by the request to "explain your selection." Items were judged to be correct (a score of one) if the correct answer and an adequate explanation or set of calculations demonstrating understanding of the underlying reasoning pattern involved. If the answer was determined to be incorrect, it was given a score of zero.

### Graphing skill

Subjects were pre- and post-tested on knowledge of standard graphing technique using eight questions from a modified version of the Test of Graphing in Science by McKenzie and Padilla (1986), which has been found to have criterion validity and to measure one broad construct (graphing ability). Questions include those that require students to select appropriately scaled set of axes, select the best fit line, locate the corresponding point on a graph when given a set of coordinates, select the correct graph when given a description of an investigation and/or a completed data table, and interpolate and/or extrapolate to identify trends in a given graph.

### Attitudes

The attitudinal pre- and post-test consisted of 16 questions using a Likert scale from one (strongly disagree) to five (strongly agree) regarding student attitudes toward biology and modes of learning. Sixteen attitudinal items were factor analyzed using the principal components method with a varimax rotation. Based on this analysis, three additive scales were formed based on factor analysis of the questionnaire—attitudes toward working in groups (rather than individually), attitudes toward using computers to learn, and a combination of interest in biology and confidence in ability to succeed in biology. Preference for choosing another instructor if the student had the option of "doing it again" was also analyzed.

Although the Likert scale employed is a subinterval scale, Gardner (1975) persuasively argues that employing parametric statistical procedures with subinterval scales leads to credible results when a large sample size such as ours is employed. Thus ANOVA, a parametric statistical procedure, was used to analyze subjects' attitudinal scores.

## Results

Based on post-tests, online students were as successful as on-campus students at acquiring an understanding of biology content, acquiring graphing skill, increasing reasoning ability, and developing positive attitudes toward science.

### Knowledge of biology

In this study ANOVA detected no significant difference on final examination means between online classes (M = 32.57) and the on-campus class (M = 31.15). As shown in Table 1, ANOVA also indicated no significant difference in course grades for online (M = 81.86) and on-campus classes (M = 78.46).

As shown in table 2, students reported no significant difference in the number of biology courses previously completed (online M = 2.18, on-campus M = 2.08). However ANOVA indicated online students demonstrated somewhat higher scores on the biology pretest. The mean for online students was 5.59 while the mean for on-campus students was 4.84 ($p = .05$).

### Reasoning level

As shown in Table 1, ANOVA detected no significant difference in means for reasoning post-test scores between online (M = 9.66) and on-campus (M = 8.56) classes. However, when students were categorized as concrete (zero to three correct answers), transitional (four to seven correct), or formal reasoners (more than seven correct), Chi square analysis revealed a statistically significant difference between online and on-campus students.

Two percent of online students were classified as concrete, 5 percent as transitional reasoners, and 93 percent as formal reasoners. In contrast, 6 percent of on-campus students were classified as concrete, 24 percent as transitional, and 71 percent as formal reasoners [$\chi^2$ (2, n =76) = 6.74, $p$ =.03.] Percentages were rounded to the nearest whole percent.

Both ANOVA and Chi square analysis detected statistically higher pretest reasoning levels for online students (Table 2). The mean for online students was 7.80 as compared to 6.38 for on-campus students ($p$ = .01). Based on pretest performance, 11 percent of online students were classified as concrete reasoners, 26 percent as transitional reasoners, and 64 percent as formal reasoners. In contrast, 21 percent of on-campus students were classified as concrete, 40 percent as transitional, and 38 percent as formal reasoners [$\chi^2$ (2, n =113) = 7.25, $p$ =.03].

**Graphing skill**

As shown in Table 1, ANOVA indicated no significant difference in post-test graphing skill for online (M = 7.35) and on-campus classes (M = 6.77). Analysis of data in Table 2 shows that online students had somewhat higher pretest scores of graphing skill. The mean for online

## Table 1.
### Dependent variables by instructional method

| | Mean Online (SD) N=66 | Mean On-campus (SD) N=50 | df | F | Prob.* |
|---|---|---|---|---|---|
| Course Grade (%) | 81.86  (10.19) | 78.46  (1.54) | 1 | 2.39 | .13 |
| Final Examination (50 possible) | 32.57  (6.01) | 31.15  (6.94) | 1 | .94 | .34 |
| Graphing Skill (8 possible) | 7.35  (.84) | 6.77  (1.31) | 1 | 2.35 | .13 |
| Reasoning Level (12 possible) | 9.66  (2.04) | 8.56  (2.89) | 1 | 3.70 | .06 |
| Att. - Like Group Work (10 max.) ^ | 4.98  (1.93) | 7.23  (2.22) | 1 | 22.87 | .00 |
| Att. - Bio Interesting/ Confidence (25 max.) | 16.57  (3.67) | 17.29  (3.58) | 1 | .74 | .39 |
| Att. - Like Using Computers (10 max.) | 8.56  (1.58) | 6.43  (2.13) | 1 | 25.66 | .00 |
| Att. - Satisfaction with Instructor (5 max.) | 4.47  (.74) | 4.29  (1.10) | 1 | .74 | .39 |
| | Online (n) | On-campus (n) | df | $\chi^2$ | Prob. |
| Withdrawal Rate | 32%** (21) | 27% (13) | 1 | .30 | .59 |
| Reasoning Level | | | 2 | 6.74 | .03 |
|    Concrete Reasoner | 2%  (1) | 6%  (2) | | | |
|    Transitional Reasoner | 5%  (2) | 24%  (8) | | | |
|    Formal Reasoner | 93%  (39) | 71%  (24) | | | |

* Values have been rounded to two decimal places so that .00 indicates a value of .005 or less.
^ Att. stands for attitude.
** Percentages have been rounded to the nearest whole number.

classes was 6.14 while the mean for the on-campus class was 5.51 ($p = .05$).

### Attitudes

Attitudinal preferences were measured on a Likert scale from one "strongly disagree" to five "strongly agree". Scores were recoded where necessary so that higher scores reflected positive attitudes toward the particular construct being measured.

ANOVA indicated no significant difference in pre-or post-attitudes between online and on-campus students for interest in biology and confidence in ability to succeed in biology (pretest online M = 17.18, pretest on-campus M = 17.80; post-test online M = 16.57, post-test on-campus M = 17.29). There was also no significant difference in satisfaction with instructor. The means for choosing the same instructor if the student had the option of "doing it again" was 4.47 for online classes and 4.29 for the on-campus class.

As shown in Table 2, ANOVA yielded statistics that online students had significantly more favorable pretest attitudes toward using computers to learn (M = 8.71) than on-campus students (M = 7.64, $p = .00$). These attitudes were still held on post-tests (online M = 8.56, on-campus M = 6.43, $p = .00$).

Online students also expressed significantly less favorable pretest attitudes toward working in a group (M = 5.71) than on-campus students (M = 6.88, $p = .00$)). These attitudes were also expressed on post-tests (online M = 4.98, on-campus M = 7.23, $p = .00$)).

### Designing a controlled experiment

The weekly bulletin board asked students to describe in detail one of the experiments they conducted. In the first few weeks of the semester, very few online students are able to apply the knowledge gained from reading about the need to control variables to their experimental design. For example, the first online laboratory experiment directs students to gather evidence as to what factors affect the behavior of animals such as earthworms, crickets, or goldfish (Fig. 1). Students are advised to investigate the effect of light, temperature, types of soil, types of food, etc. Students frequently change two or three variables at once. They may move the animals from the light to the dark, set the container holding the animals on a heating pad (rather than leaving it at room temperature), and add a cotton ball soaked in vinegar to a container that previously housed only the animals being studied.

The instructor poses follow-up bulletin board questions as to whether the conclusions the students reached are reasonable given the experimental protocol. The focus initially is on the inappropriateness of changing several variables at once. As the semester progresses, weekly bulletin board postings reveal a steady improvement in the ability of most students to design and conduct controlled experiments. Students quickly recognize in postings of their colleagues when variables have not been controlled and alert the student to the problem.

This progression of knowledge is very similar, if not identical, to that seen in on-campus students who do the same experiment the first week of the semester. Their in-class discussions closely resemble those seen on the bulletin board.

### Identifying causal relationships

The ability of students to evaluate evidence supporting or refuting a causal relationship between independent and dependent variables are similar to that described above. Bulletin board postings and in-class discussions early in the semester are quite unsatisfactory in this regard. As the semester progresses, however, students in both online and on-campus classes acquire this skill. The instructor noted no differences between online and on-campus classes in either the number of students who acquired the ability to identify causal relationships or the speed at which students acquired this skill.

## Descriptive variables

As shown in Table 2, students identified their age as one of three categories: 20 years or less, 21 to 30 years, or over 30 years. There was a statistically significant difference in the two groups, with the online classes being composed of more older students and the on-campus class with younger students [$\chi^2$ (2, n =116) = 11.35, $p$ =. 00]. Seventeen percent of online students were in the 20 or under age group, while 64 percent were 21 to 30 years and 20 percent were over 30. Forty-four percent of on-campus students were in the 20 or under age group, while 48 percent were 21 to 30 years, and 8 percent were over 30.

Students identified their race as to Caucasian or minority (African American, Asian American, Hispanic, or Native American). Although there was a higher percentage of minority students on-campus (22 percent) than online (12 percent), the difference was not statistically significant [$\chi^2$ (1, n =116) = 2.03, $p$ =. 16].

## Table 2.
### Pretest and descriptive variables by instructional method

| | Mean Online (SD) N=66 | | Mean On-campus (SD) N=50 | | df | F | Prob. |
|---|---|---|---|---|---|---|---|
| Previous Biology Courses | 2.18 | (.58) | 2.08 | (.67) | 1 | .80 | .37 |
| Biology Pretest (14 possible) | 5.59 | (2.20) | 4.84 | (1.66) | 1 | 4.03 | .05 |
| Graphing Pretest (8 possible) | 6.14 | (1.67) | 5.51 | (1.61) | 1 | 4.07 | .05 |
| Reasoning Level (12 possible) | 7.80 | (2.89) | 6.38 | (2.89) | 1 | 6.61 | .01 |
| Att. - Like Group Work (10 max.) | 5.71 | (1.75) | 6.88 | (2.13) | 1 | 10.51 | .00 |
| Att. - Bio Interesting/ Confidence (25 max.) | 17.18 | (2.66) | 17.80 | (3.29) | 1 | 1.23 | .27 |
| Att. - Like Using Computers (10 max.) | 8.71 | (1.58) | 7.64 | (1.69) | 1 | 12.38 | .00 |
| | Online (n) | | On-campus (n) | | df | $\chi^2$ | Prob. |
| Reasoning Level: | | | | | 2 | 7.25 | .03 |
| Concrete Reasoner | 11% | (7) | 21% | (10) | | | |
| Transitional Reasoner | 26% | (17) | 40% | (19) | | | |
| Formal Reasoner | 64% | (42) | 38% | (18) | | | |
| Age: | | | | | 2 | 11.35 | .00 |
| 20 or under | 17% | (11) | 44% | (22) | | | |
| 21 to 30 years | 64% | (42) | 48% | (24) | | | |
| over 30 years | 20% | (13) | 8% | (4) | | | |
| Race: | | | | | 1 | 2.03 | .16 |
| Caucasian | 88% | (58) | 78% | (39) | | | |
| Minority | 12% | (8) | 22% | (11) | | | |
| Gender: | | | | | 1 | .00 | .97 |
| Male | 36% | (24) | 36% | (18) | | | |
| Female | 64% | (42) | 64% | (32) | | | |

There was no difference between online students and on-campus students for gender. Both groups were 64 percent female and 36 percent male.

**Withdrawal rate**

As shown in Table 1, there was no statistically significant difference in withdrawal rates between online students and on-campus students. Online classes had a 32 percent withdrawal rate while the on-campus class had a 27 percent withdrawal rate [$\chi^2$ (1, n =114) = .30, p =. 59].

## Discussion

This study found that there were no statistically significant differences in outcomes for students in online and on-campus biology classes. Course grades provide an instructor-generated measure of student learning. Because assigning course grades may involve subjective judgment and the teacher may "teach to the test."

In this study, the final examination student was a noninstructor-generated instrument that the instructor did not view before administration. Although the mean was lower than hoped for, it was equal to that of on-campus students in a similar inquiry-based class. In a previous study, on-campus inquiry-based students were found to score significantly higher ( M = 31.32) than on-campus expository students ( M = 27.68, p = .00) on this same final examination (Johnson, 1993).

Ideally, all college students should be formal reasoners—able to reason with many, if not most abstract concepts. This would empower them to grasp the abstract concepts integral to their coursework and to their daily lives. Because students who pretested as transitional reasoners are able to reason abstractly with some concepts, they may be the most amenable to further development of reasoning ability. It is notable that approximately one-third of the online and on-campus students in this study moved from transitional reasoners to formal reasoners.

Based on the data in this study, graphing skill improved in both online and on-campus students.

The mean for both groups increased by at least one (out of a possible score of eight).

Students in both groups continued to express relatively positive attitudes about biology and their instructor. Because the students in the online class are a self-selected group, it was expected that they would express significantly more favorable attitudes toward using computers to learn and less favorable toward working in groups and they did.

As evidenced by the progression of bulletin board discussions, online students appeared to duplicate the experience of on-campus students in gradually developing the ability to design and conduct controlled experiments as well as identify causal relationships between independent and dependent variables.

Although online students withdrew at a slightly higher rate than on-campus students, it was not statistically significant. Many online students reported extremely heavy workloads coupled with family commitments and course work as the reason they chose the flexibility of an online course. When these factors are coupled with the increased demands for independent learning, time-management skills, and self-discipline required of an online student, perhaps it is not surprising that more decide to withdraw. They find themselves overcommitted, despite the flexibility of the online format.

While we believe these results are representative and informative, the reader should be aware this is a quasi-experimental design because students were not randomly assigned to treatment group. The textbook was not the same for the two groups. Results for the online and on-campus classes are from different semesters. While the content of the courses, the instructor, and the learning objectives were constant, it is possible that other unidentified variables may have influenced outcomes.

It is possible that instrument decay could have influenced student performance. If knowledge of the pretests, post-tests, quizzes, and/or examinations somehow leaked out, students would be expected to score higher on these measures. To prevent such an occurrence, students did not receive feedback on any of their answers on the pre- or post-tests in any semester. Questions on the reasoning post-test measured the same constructs as the reasoning pretest, but slightly different questions were used. Midterm and final examinations were never returned to students although grades were posted for these measurements. Although students in one semester of online classes could print their online quizzes and pass them onto students in subsequent semesters, a significant number of questions were changed in each quiz from semester to semester. For individual students, his or her grades on the midterm and final examination (measures that could not be shared from one semester to another) correlated well with his or her online quiz average. Thus, it appears unlikely that instrument decay significantly affected the results of this study.

Online students had statistically significant higher biology pretest scores, reasoning levels, and graphing skills. Students electing to enroll in an online laboratory science course have judged themselves capable of learning the necessary concepts in an educational setting that is likely to require working more independently, better time management skills, and more self-discipline than the equivalent course on-campus. This study does not provide evidence regarding the success of more poorly prepared and/or motivated students in an online course.

This study provides evidence that certain types of students can learn as much biology content, develop their reasoning and graphing skills, and have as positive attitudes toward biology as those enrolled in an on-campus class. It is possible, however, that online biology classes may not serve students well who lack time-management skills, self-discipline, have lower reasoning levels, and/or weaker biology backgrounds.

**References**

Bray, H. 1999. Virtual campus. *The Boston Globe Magazine*. April 11. Online at *www.boston.com/globe/magazine/4-11/featurestory3.shtml accessed 6/00*.

Carnevale, D. 2000. U.S. lawmaker questions quality of the online-learning experience. *Chronicle of Higher Education*, A51.

Gardner, P. 1975. Scales and statistics. *Review of Educational Research* 15(1): 43-57.

Johnson, M.A. 1993. Evaluating educational outcomes with alternative methods of instruction in a non-majors college biology course. Ph.D. diss., Arizona State University.

Karplus, R. 1977. Science teaching and the development of reasoning. *Journal of Research in Science Teaching* 14:169-175.

Lawson, A.E. 1978. The development and validation of a classroom test of formal reasoning. *Journal of Research in Science Teaching* 15(1): 11-24.

Lawson, A.E. 1987. *Classroom Test of Scientific Reasoning: Revised Pencil-Paper Edition*. Tempe, AZ: Arizona State University Press.

Lawson, A.E. 1988. A better way to teach biology. *The American Biology Teacher* 50(5): 266-278.

McKenzie, D.L., and M.J. Padilla. 1986. The construction and validation of the test of graphing in science (TOGS). *Journal of Research in Science Teaching* 23(7): 571-579.

Noble, D.F. 1998. Digital diploma mills: The automation of higher education. *First Monday* 3(1). Online at *www.firstmonday.dk/issues/issue3_1/noble/index.html accessed 5/00*.

# Appendix A

*Resource List*

Some Particularly Rich Websites for Two-Year College Teachers

## The League for Innovation in the Community College
*www.league.org/index.html#projects*
**From their Website:** The League is an international service consortium dedicated to catalyzing the community college movement. More than 750 institutions have joined our efforts, and we partner with more than 100 corporations. You can learn more about the League through this website and by signing up for our digital newsletter.

## The American Association of Community Colleges
*www.aacc.nche.edu*
**From their Website:** The American Association of Community Colleges is the primary advocacy organization for the nation's community colleges. The Association represents more than 1,100 associate degree-granting institutions and some 10 million students. Formed in 1920, AACC is a national voice for community colleges, which marked their 100th year of service to the nation in 2001. AACC is leading the celebration of the colleges as they provide learning opportunities to their students and communities and the nation.

## Information Resources for Community Colleges
*www.mcli.dist.maricopa.edu/cc/gen.html*
**From their Website:** According to latest statistics from the American Association of Community Colleges (AACC), there are 1,166 community colleges in the United States. This site contains a searchable index to the websites for **1304** community colleges in the United States, Canada, and elsewhere around the world. The interface we set up allows you to search **alphabetically** (by the first letter of the college's name), **geographically** (by the country/state/province), or by **keywords** in the college name, location, or web address.

# Appendix B

## NSTA Convention Schedule

(All cities are subject to change pending final negotiation.)
NSTA Conventions are great places to meet other two-year-college science teachers, share stories and ideas, and attend demonstrations, workshops, and seminars.

### National Conventions
- Atlanta, GA: April 1-4, 2004
- Dallas, TX: March 31-April 3, 2005
- Anaheim, CA: April 6-9, 2006
- New Orleans, LA: April 12-15, 2007
- Boston, MA: March 27-30, 2008
- Indianapolis, IN: April 2-5, 2009
- Washington, DC: March 18-21, 2010
- San Francisco, CA: April 7-10, 2011

### Area Conventions

**2003 Area Conventions**
- North/Midwestern - Minneapolis, MN: Oct. 30-Nov. 1
- South/Midwestern - Kansas City, MO: November 13-15
- Western - Reno, NV: December 4-6

**2004 Area Conventions**
- Northeastern - Indianapolis, IN: November 4-6
- Northwestern - Seattle, WA: November 18-20
- Eastern - Richmond, VA: December 2-4

**2005 Area Conventions**
- TBD
- Northeastern - Chicago, IL: November 10-12
- Southern - Nashville, TN: December 1-3

**2006 Area Conventions**
- Northwestern - Omaha, NE: October 19-21
- TBD
- Southwestern - Phoenix, AZ: December 7-9

**2007 Area Conventions**
- North/Midwestern - Detroit, MI: October 18-20
- Western - Denver, CO: November 15-17
- Southern - Birmingham, AL: December 6-8

# Appendix C

## List of Contributors

(in alphabetical order)

**Debra S. Borgesen** is a co-author of "Teaching to Learn: Why Should Teachers Have All the Fun?"

**Bruno Borsari** is an assistant professor of agroecology, Department of Parks and Recreation/Environmental Education, at Slippery Rock University of Pennsylvania. He is author of "A Practical Application of Andragogical Theory Assumptions in Introductory Biology Courses" and "Teaching Introductory Agriculture Courses Through Distance Education Technology at Louisiana State University."

**Mario Caprio** served as editor of the two-year college department of the *Journal of College Science Teachers* for ten years. He is author or co-author of numerous articles in this compendium, including "Hello! Is Anybody Out There?," "Adjunct Faculty," "Navigating the Standards," "Designing Nonmajors' Science Courses," "Teaching to Learn: Why Should Teachers Have All the Fun?," "A Path Toward Integrated Science," "Chaos and Opportunity," and "Getting There from Here." He is Professor Emeritus at Suffolk Community College, in Selden, New York. Dr. Caprio is currently developing a laboratory program and coordinating nonmajors biology laboratories at Tennessee Technological University, in Cookeville, Tennessee.

**Christine L. Case**, co-author of "The Antimicrobial Properties of Red Algae," is a biology professor at Skyline College in San Bruno, California.

**Diane Cheatwood**, one of the authors of the article "Adjunct Faculty," is an Educational Consultant in Aurora, Colorado.

**Frances T. Costa** is one of the authors of the article "Adjunct Faculty."

**Marjorie M. Cowan**, co-author of "The First Day of Class on a Two-Year College Campus," is associate professor of microbiology, Miami University in Ohio.

**Nathan Dubowsky** is one of the authors of the articles "Adjunct Faculty" and "The Graying of Science Faculty in U.S. Colleges and Universities." He is professor of biology at Westchester Community College in Valhalla, New York.

**Ken Garver** is the author of the article "A Computerized Approach to Mastery Learning." He is professor of biological sciences at Victor Valley Community College in Victorville, California.

**Susan Harriman**, instructor of physics at Volunteer State Community College in Gallatin, Tennessee, is one of the authors of "A Path Toward Integrated Science—The First Steps."

**Elliott Hartman, Jr.** is a professor in the Physical Science Department at Westchester Community College in Valhalla, New York. He is a co-author of "The Graying of Science Faculty in U.S. Colleges and Universities."

**James E. Heath, Jr.**, author of "A Two-Sided Mirror of Science Education," teaches at Austin Community College in Austin, Texas.

**James A. Hewlett**, associate professor of biology at Finger Lakes Community College in Canandaigua, New York, is author of "Trouble in Paradise: A Case of Speciation."

**Art Hobson** is the author of "Designing Science Literacy Courses." He is Professor Emeritus of physics at the University of Arkansas in Fayetteville.

**Margaret Johnson** is the author of "Introductory Biology *Online:* Assessing Outcomes of Two Student Populations." She is professor of biology and microbiology at Mesa Community College in Mesa, Arizona.

**Jeffrey D. Kent**, associate professor of biology at Volunteer State Community College in Gallatin, Tennessee, is one of the authors of "A Path Toward Integrated Science—The First Steps."

**George S. Lomaga**, co-author of "Screening Potential Laboratory Telecourse Students," teaches in the Earth/Space Science Department at Suffolk County Community College in Selden, New York.

**Thomas R. Lord** is author of "Are We Cultivating 'Couch Potatoes' in Our College Science Courses?" He is a biology professor at Indiana University of Pennsylvania, in Indiana, Pennsylvania.

**Eddie Lunsford** is author of the article "Inquiry in the Community College Biology Lab." He is an adjunct science instructor at Southwestern Community College in Sylva, North Carolina.

**Lynda B. Micikas**, co-author of "Getting There from Here," works for the Biological Sciences Curriculum Study (BSCS) in Colorado Springs, Colorado.

**Chris E. Petersen**, professor in the Natural Sciences Department at College of DuPage in Glen Ellyn, Illinois, is author of the article "An Experimental Project Approach to Biology."

**K.W. Piepgrass** is co-author of "The First Day of Class on a Two-Year College Campus."

**Parris Powers**, associate professor of chemistry at Volunteer State Community College in Gallatin, Tennessee, is one of the authors of "A Path Toward Integrated Science—The First Steps."

**Jerry Przybylski**, one of the authors of "The Graying of Science Faculty in U.S. Colleges and Universities," is an associate professor of biology at Elmira College in Elmira, New York.

**Leonard Simons**, one of the authors of "The Graying of Science Faculty in U.S. Colleges and Universities," is a biology professor at Elmira College in Elmira, New York.

**Charles Snelling**, instructor of chemistry at Volunteer State Community College in Gallatin, Tennessee, is one of the authors of "A Path Toward Integrated Science—The First Steps."

**Kathleen Lillo Sowell**, author of "The Counseling/Science Connection," is a counselor at Volunteer State Community College in Gallatin, Tennessee.

**Ethel D. Stanley** is co-author of *"LifeLines OnLine:* Curriculum and Teaching Strategies for Adult Learners." She is the Director of BioQUEST at Beloit College, Beloit, Wisconsin.

**Robert L. Warasila** is a professor in the Physical Sciences Department at Suffolk County Community College in Selden, New York. He is a co-author of "Adjunct Faculty" and "Screening Potential Laboratory Telecourse Students."

**Michael Warner** is co-author of "The Antimicrobial Properties of Red Algae."

**Margaret A. Waterman** is co-author of *"LifeLines OnLine:* Curriculum and Teaching Strategies for Adult Learners." She is an associate professor of biology at Southeast Missouri State University in Cape Girardeau, Missouri.

# Index

Page numbers in **boldface** type indicate figures or tables.

scientific paper, 83–84

student engagement in, 81–82

First day of class, 5–8, **7**

Guided inquiry, 92

# K

# L

Mailing lists on Internet, 3–4
Mentoring programs, 16–17, 21

National Research Council (NRC), 33–34, 87
*National Science Education Standards (NSES)*, 33–34, 37–38, 39, 40
National Science Foundation (NSF), 87, 98, 101
National Science Teachers Association (NSTA) conventions, 141
Noble, David F., 131
NRC (National Research Council), 33–34, 87
*NSES (National Science Education Standards)*, 33–34, 37–38, 39, 40
NSF (National Science Foundation), 87, 98, 101
NSTA (National Science Teachers Association) conventions, 141

Open inquiry, 92
Orientation programs, 16

PBL (Problem-Based Learning), 104
PC University software, 119
Pedagogy, 53
Peer coaching, 78–79
Peer instruction, 45, 47
Problem-Based Learning (PBL), 104
Professional development activities, 17–18
Professional development centers, 79
Professional societies, 79
Purposeful inquiry, 92

Question Bank software, 118